KUMON READING WORKBOOKS

4

Reading

Table of Contents

1 Read the passage. Then answer the questions below using only words from the passage.

11 points per question

Gavin wanted to be on the track team very badly. He thought about it for weeks before tryouts began. He was restless and spent days walking around the house looking for something to do. Just when he thought the wait would be endless, that beautiful spring day arrived. It was time for tryouts!

He was nervous. Would he be at his fastest? Or would he at least be fast enough to make the team? Everyone at the tryouts looked bigger and stronger than he was. He looked at his competition nervously. When it was time to race, Gavin swiftly took his place in the starting blocks. There was no more time to think. It was finally time to run.

(1) How badly did Gavin want to be on the track team?

Gavin wanted to be on the track team _____, and he thought about it for _____.

(2) How did Gavin feel while he was walking around the house?

Gavin felt _____ while he was walking around the house.

(3) What was the first question Gavin asked himself at the tryouts?

Gavin asked himself if he would be at his _____.

(4) How did everyone at the tryouts look?

Everyone at the tryouts looked _____ than Gavin.

(5) What did Gavin do when it was time to race?

When it was time to race, Gavin _____ took his place in the starting blocks.

2 Choose the correct word pair from the box to complete each sentence.

4 points per question

useful / useless	heavy / heavier	swift / swiftly
cheerful / cheerfully	careful / careless	big / biggest

(1) Though our pumpkin was _____, it did not win the prize for _____ pumpkin.

(2) Jane has a favorite pair of scissors that she thinks are very _____.
Her sister has a pair that she left in the rain and are rusty and _____.

(3) That bird is _____. Look how _____ it flew to the ground!

(4) I packed a _____ suitcase, but my mother's was five pounds _____.

(5) My doctor is very _____, but sometimes I wish he didn't talk so _____ when I am sick.

(6) Riding your bike can be dangerous if you are _____.
It's better to be _____.

3 Draw a line to match the words below with their opposites.

3 points per question

(1) uphill •——————————————————• ⓐ unhappily

(2) colorful •   • ⓑ noisier

(3) quickly •   • ⓒ downhill

(4) roughest •   • ⓓ oldest

(5) youngest •   • ⓔ slowly

(6) happily •   • ⓕ smoothest

(7) quieter •   • ⓖ colorless

We're just getting started!

Vocabulary

2

Level ☆

Score

Date / /

Name

/100

1 Read the passage. Then complete the exercises below.

Did you know the average American citizen creates up to four-and-a-half pounds of trash per day? That's almost a ton of trash per year! Americans create an unbelievable amount of trash. Being very wasteful can cause ①_____ in our landfills. What can we do about having too much trash?

There are many different things we can do to reduce the amount of trash we make. The most popular way is to ②_____. When we recycle, we send our used plastic, rubber, metal and paper items to a plant where the products are broken down into basic materials for future products. Did you know that recycled rubber is used for playground mats?

Another important way to reduce, however, is to reuse. Instead of going to the supermarket and choosing between paper and plastic bags, how about bringing your own ③_____ bags with you? Bags that you can use again and again don't create any trash!

(1) Complete the passage using the vocabulary words defined below.

10 points per question

overcrowding	too populated by objects or people
reusable	something that is able to be used again
recycle	breaking down products into basic objects for use in future products

(2) Complete the statements below using words from the passage only.

10 points per question

① How much trash does the average American citizen create per day?

The average American citizen creates _____

_____.

② What can being wasteful cause?

Being wasteful can cause _____.

2 Choose the correct word to complete each sentence below.

5 points per question

(1) You can easily _____ plastic bags when you go shopping.   [reuse / redo]

(2) Even with a couple of holes in this tent, it's still _____.   [usable / useless]

(3) Jen invited too many people to her party, and now her basement is

_____.   [overcrowded / underwater]

(4) Please _____ those cans for me.   [recycle / bicycle]

(5) I had an argument with my brother when he said my favorite book was

_____ and couldn't have happened.   [believable / unbelievable]

(6) After the bumpy train ride, all of the clothes in my bag were _____.

[unfolded / refolded]

3 Read the following description of an object in the picture below. Then circle the object that is described in the passage.

20 points

> The object is one of the larger things in the picture. There are taller things in the picture, but this object is the heaviest one shown. It is definitely one of the largest things in the picture. The object is reusable, and also very important for a picnic.

Let's go!

Defining Words by Context
The Science Fair

3

Level ☆

Date / /

Name

Score / 100

1 Read the passage. Then complete the exercises below.

For the science fair this fall, Mona wasn't sure what she should do. There was a ①_____ this year, and the winning project would receive a big medal and a free trip to space camp the following summer. She really wanted to be an astronaut and go into space. She thought long and hard about her entry into the contest.

Her brother was no help. He kept bouncing around the room and asking her to play a board game with him.

"This is no time for ②_____!" she said to him. "This is serious, not just fun and games!"

After he left the room, she sighed. She started to daydream. In her daydream, she had created a great ③_____, and everyone was impressed with her new idea. Crowds gathered around and asked her how she had thought of something so interesting. A big medal was handed to her, and the ④_____ read, "You're on your way to the stars!"

(1) Complete the passage using the vocabulary words defined below.

8 points per question

competition	a contest
invention	something new
recreation	fun and games
inscription	words printed or engraved on something

(2) Answer the question below using only words from the passage.

8 points

What would the winning project at the science fair receive?

The winning project would receive a _____ and a _____ _____ the following summer.

2   Answer the questions using only words from the passage below. 5 points per question

> Mona thought hard about her invention all vacation long. While her friends were playing in the sun, Mona was reading about the stars. While her brother was begging for her attention, she was watching movies about comets. After all her research, she knew she had to sit down and actually start building her project. The project was due early in the school year, so she had to start the construction of her project soon!

(1) When did Mona work on her invention?

Mona worked on her invention _____.

(2) What was her brother begging for?

Her brother was _____.

(3) What did Mona have to do after all of her research?

After all her research, Mona had to sit down and actually _____

_____.

(4) Why did Mona have to start construction soon?

Mona had to start _____ soon because the project was _____

_____.

3   Pick the correct word from the box to finish each sentence below.   8 points per question

invention	attention	competition	construction	recreation

(1) The teacher asked everyone to pay _____ while she spoke.

(2) Eliza took home first prize at the karate _____.

(3) Thomas Edison's most famous _____ was the lightbulb.

(4) When will they begin _____ on the new school?

(5) My favorite kind of _____ is basketball.

We are headed in the right direction!

Defining Words by Context
Big Top Mystery

4

Level ☆

Score ____ / 100

Date   /   /

Name

1 Read the passage. Then complete the exercises below.

The Big Top Circus had a problem on their hands. They had lost an elephant! It's a mystery how such an ①_____ animal went missing. The owner of the circus was hopping mad and demanded that a detective be sent.

The detective arrived and was clearly a good one. He looked in every single tent and went through everyone's dresser drawers. He did not rule anyone out — he even thought the owner might be a suspect. The detective was ②_____ of everyone. When he went through the clowns' clothes, a few clowns laughed. There were balloons and big clown pants flying through the air.

"This is not funny," said the detective. "This is a serious matter. There is a very large animal on the loose somewhere. An elephant can be a ③_____ animal if it is scared. It could trample people!"

Suddenly everyone was quiet. Many of the animals moved around restlessly and a clown coughed. It seemed that everyone was ④_____.

(1)   Complete the passage using the vocabulary words defined below.

8 points per question

suspicious	to have doubts about someone or something
dangerous	able or likely to inflict harm
enormous	huge
anxious	uneasy or worried

(2)   Answer the question below using only words from the passage.

8 points

What did the detective say when a few clowns laughed?

The detective said that this was not _____ and that it was a

_____.

2 Answer the questions using only words from the passage below. 5 points per question

> One of the clowns could not stop moving around. His tall hat kept falling off, and his face seemed even more red than usual. He was more nervous than the other clowns.
>
> When the detective started to move towards the clown, he tried to run. He tripped and fell over his big shoes. This time, no one laughed.
>
> The detective took him to the police station. He was curious about what the clown had to say about the missing elephant.

(1) Why did one clown's face seem more red than usual?

He was more _____ than the other clowns.

(2) What happened when the detective started to move towards him?

The clown tried to _____, but he _____

_____.

(3) Why did the detective take the clown to the police station?

The detective was _____ about what the clown had to say about the

_____.

3 Pick the correct word from the box to finish each sentence below. 9 points per question

curious	nervous	dangerous	enormous	famous

(1) I was _____ that I didn't study enough for the test, but I did well.

(2) Cheetahs might look cute, but they are very _____ animals.

(3) Jorge wants to be a _____ singer one day.

(4) The Grand Canyon is an _____ canyon.

(5) Our cat is very _____ and is always exploring strange places.

I am scared of clowns!

Vocabulary Review

5

Level ☆

Date   /   /

Name

Score

/100

1 Unscramble the words below to finish the sentences.

5 points per question

(1)   I was late, so I _____ grabbed my things and left.   [if / tly / sw]

(2)   Always remember to _____ your bottles and cans!   [cy / re / cle]

(3)   The person in line behind us is a _____ actress!   [us / mo / fa]

(4)   Riding a bike without a helmet is _____.   [us / ro / ge / dan]

(5)   The telephone was a very important _____.   [ve / in / nt / ion]

(6)   When will they begin _____ on the new museum?

[on / ti / co / ns / uc / tr]

2 Read the sentences. Then choose a word in bold from one of the sentences to match each definition below.

6 points per question

-- Since I knew I would be getting paid, I mowed the lawn **cheerfully**.

-- Chauncey was very **anxious** about speaking in front of the class.

-- Lunch time was a time for **recreation**.

-- The **science** of biology is very interesting to me.

-- Using **reusable** bags is good for the environment.

(1)   recreation   fun and games

(2)   _____   done in a way that is full of spirit and happiness

(3)   _____   something that is able to be used again

(4)   _____   knowledge covering general truths about a subject

(5)   _____   uneasy or worried

3 Complete the crossword puzzle using the sentences below as clues. Use capital letters.

5 points per question

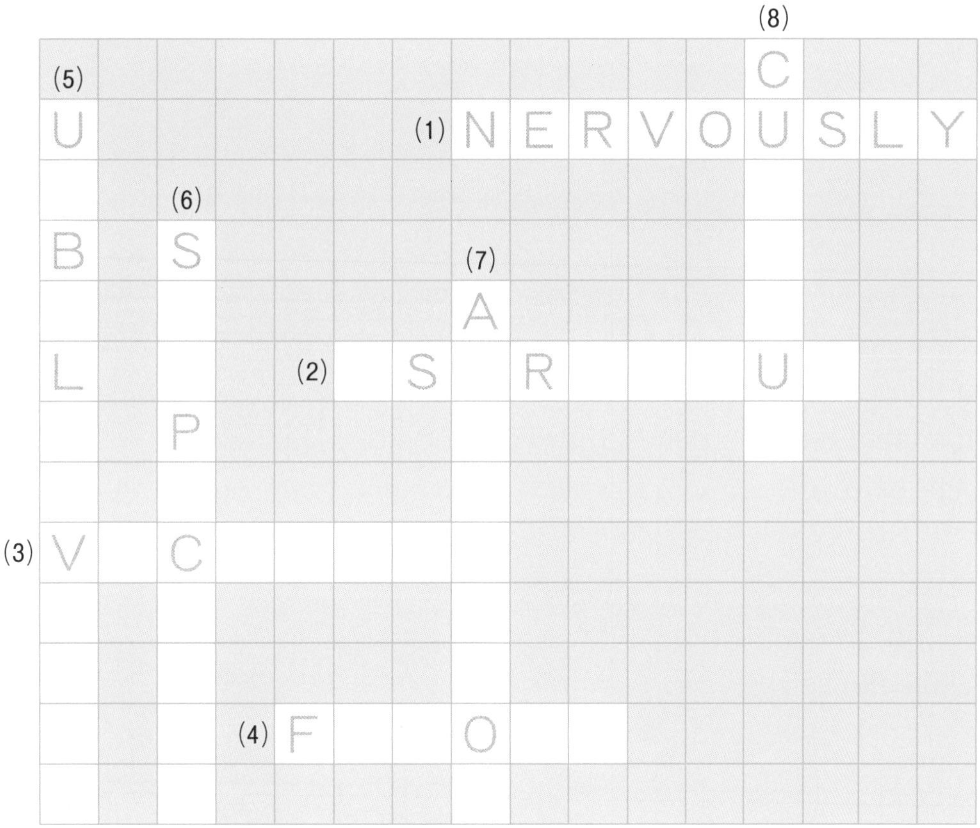
(8) C
(5) U
(1) NERVOUSLY
(6) B S
(7) A
L (2) S R U
P
(3) V C
(4) F O

ACROSS

(1) While I was waiting for my test score, I tapped my desk __?__.

(2) The __?__ got into his suit in preparation for the launch into space.

(3) Jane couldn't wait for summer __?__ any longer.

(4) Eliza wants to be a __?__ writer some day.

DOWN

(5) __?__ things happen in movies all the time.

(6) My brother always gets __?__ of me when I'm in his room.

(7) The teacher asked Matt to sit up and pay __?__ in class.

(8) Our cat is very __?__. He always gets his nose into things.

Good job!

6

Who/What/When/Where/Why/How
Coins and the Mint

Level ☆☆

Date   /   /

Name

Score   /100

1 Read the following passage. Then answer the questions below using words from the passage.

10 points per question

Do you have coins in your pocket? People use coins every day. You may use coins to purchase things at the store. A clerk at the store may give you change when you make a purchase. Sometimes this change may be bills, but often it will be pennies, nickels, dimes, or quarters. You may even get a half-dollar or dollar coin. But do you know where these coins come from? The United States Mint makes all of the nation's coin currency. Only the Mint may make coin currency. Without the Mint, we would not have the coins that we use to purchase things.

Coins were once more common than paper money. In fact, the first real dollars were coins, not bills. Early lawmakers knew the United States would need its own coins. They decided to create the Mint. The Mint opened in 1792 in Philadelphia, which was then the nation's capital. Now the Mint has six locations. Only the locations in Philadelphia and Denver make the currency we use every day.

(1) Where may coins be made in the United States?

Coin currency can be made only at the _____.

(2) What were the first real dollars?

The first real dollars were _____.

(3) Why did lawmakers decide to create the Mint?

Lawmakers decided to create the Mint because they knew the United States would

_____.

(4) When did the Mint first open?

The Mint first opened in _____.

2 Read the passage. Then answer the questions below using words from the passage.

12 points per question

You can visit the Mint in Denver or Philadelphia in order to see how coins are made. The first Mint had trouble making enough coins for the country. Now the Philadelphia and Denver locations make between 65 and 80 million coins a day! Making the nation's coin currency is a lot of work. The machines at the Philadelphia location work 24 hours a day.

U.S. coins are made from mixtures of metals such as copper or nickel. Coins are engraved with pictures on both sides. Sometimes new pictures are made for coins. New coins can be created, too. The Mint has a team of designers who engrave new pictures for coins. First the designers draw a picture. Then they make a model using a computer, and finally the machines help make the coins.

One side of a coin is usually engraved with a picture of a famous historical person. Often this is a U.S. president. You may know that the penny has a picture of President Lincoln. Not all of the pictures engraved on coins are of presidents, though. Susan B. Anthony fought for women's voting rights. Her picture is engraved on the most famous silver dollar.

(1) What was wrong with the first Mint?

The first Mint had _____ making enough _____.

(2) Why do the machines in Philadelphia work 24 hours a day?

The machines in Philadelphia work 24 hours a day because making the nation's _____ is a lot of work.

(3) What are coins made from?

Coins are made from _____ such as copper or nickel.

(4) How do designers make engravings for coins?

They draw a _____, then they make a _____ using a computer.

(5) What is usually engraved on one side of a coin?

A picture of a _____

is usually engraved on one side of a coin.

What is your favorite coin?

Who/What/When/Where/Why/How
A Fair Solution

7

Level ☆☆

Date   /   /

Name

Score

/100

1 Read the following passage. Then answer the questions below using words from the passage.

10 points per question

Jim's parents believe that everyone should participate in the housework. Everyone in Jim's family has his own chores to do. Jim's father mops the floor and does the laundry. Jim's mother cooks dinner and mows the lawn. Jim's sister Patty shovels the driveway and sweeps the porch.

Jim's job is to take garbage out every Wednesday. His family recycles their cans and bottles. This way the materials in the cans and bottles can be reused. Since his family recycles, he has to take out the cans and bottles, too. Jim doesn't mind taking out the cans and bottles, but he does not like to take out the garbage.

Jim's mother said that he didn't have to take out the garbage. "But we have to find a fair solution," she said. Jim said that he would like to cook instead of taking out the trash. "You can help me cook dinner twice a week. Then I will take out the trash twice a month," said his mother. Patty told Jim that he could help her shovel the driveway. "Then I will take out the trash twice a month, too." What a great solution! Now Jim can learn to cook, and he only has to take out the cans and bottles.

(1) What do Jim's parents believe?

Jim's parents believe that _____ in the housework.

(2) When does Jim take out the garbage?

Jim takes the garbage out _____.

(3) What does Jim not like to do?

Jim does not like _____.

(4) Who told Jim that he can help shovel the driveway?

_____ told Jim that he could help her _____.

2 Read the passage. Then answer the questions below using words from the passage.

12 points per question

Jim's mother was happy that he wanted to participate in making dinner. "Cooking is an important skill, and it can be fun!" she told him cheerfully.

"Let's make pasta and tomato sauce," said his mother. But after she checked in the pantry, she saw that there was only one can of tomatoes. This was a problem because her recipe needed two cans. "What do you think we should do?" she asked.

"Maybe we should make less pasta so that we will need less sauce. We can have more vegetables on the side to make up for the pasta," said Jim. His mother said this was a great solution.

Jim's mother showed him how to cook the tomatoes, but she told him he could only use the stove with her help. Together, they chopped the garlic and onions. Jim's mother poured the olive oil from a measuring cup. Jim stirred in the oil with the tomatoes, garlic, and onions.

When it was time to clean up, Jim knew what to do with the tomato can. He put the can in the recycling bag. On Wednesday, he would bring all the bottles and cans to the curb to be recycled.

(1) When did Jim's mother see there was only one can of tomatoes?
Jim's mother saw there was only one can of tomatoes when she _____

_____.

(2) Why was it a problem that Jim's mother found only one can of tomatoes?
This was a problem because _____.

(3) What is Jim's solution to the problem?
Jim's solution was that they should _____ so that they

needed _____.

(4) How does Jim's mother say he may use the stove?
Jim's mother told him he could only _____.

(5) What will Jim do with the bottles and cans?
Jim will bring all the bottles and cans _____.

Do you help your parents cook dinner? It's fun!

Who/What/When/Where/Why/How
Band Practice

8

Level ☆☆

Date   /   /

Name

Score   /100

1 Read the following passage. Then answer the questions below using words from the passage.

10 points per question

Claire plays the trombone in the school band. She likes the trombone because it can make very low notes. Claire's friend Paul plays the tuba. The tuba can make an even lower sound than the trombone! Claire and Paul sit with the rest of the brass section. Claire loves hearing the melody of a song played by the trumpets. Claire's friend Lyle plays the drums. Lyle can't play a melody on the drums, but he keeps the beat well.

Claire's sister Lisa plays in the band, too. Lisa likes to play high notes, so she plays the flute. She sits with the flute players near the clarinet section. Clarinets and flutes are both woodwind instruments. Woodwind and brass instruments make sound when a player blows air into the instrument.

In the spring, the band entertains the school with a concert. Sometimes the band participates in competitions with other school bands. The bands compete against each other to see who plays the best music. Claire is always a little nervous at the beginning of a competition, but hearing the melody around her always makes her relax.

(1) Why does Claire like the trombone?

Claire likes the trombone because it can _____.

(2) What sound can the tuba make?

The tuba can make an _____ than the trombone.

(3) Who likes to play high notes?

Claire's _____ likes to play high notes.

(4) How does a woodwind instrument make sound?

Woodwind instruments make a sound when a player _____ them.

(5) When does the band entertain the school with a concert?

The band entertains the school with a concert _____.

2 Read the following passage. Then answer the questions below using words from the passage.

10 points per question

Claire likes playing in the school band, but there is something she likes even more. Claire loves to hear a swinging jazz melody! Last year, Claire heard the school jazz band play in a concert. The jazz band had brass instruments, saxophones, and even a piano. She saw how much fun other students had listening to the jazz band. Kids were dancing to the melodies and tapping their feet to the swinging beat. Claire loves entertaining others. She realized the jazz band was where she belongs.

Claire wants to play trombone in the jazz band, but now she is nervous. Claire will need to compete with other trombone players for a spot. Claire knows that she cannot let being nervous stop her. She practices jazz songs every Tuesday afternoon with Lyle. He plays drums in the jazz band. Lyle told Claire that she needed to practice before competing for a spot. If she practiced, she would be less nervous when she tried out. Practicing so much takes time, but Claire knows the hard work will pay off when she is in the jazz band. After all, she was born to entertain!

(1) What were kids doing while listening to the jazz band?

Kids were _____ and _____ _____ to the swinging beat.

(2) What instruments does the jazz band have?

The jazz band has _____, saxophones, and even a _____.

(3) Why does Claire realize jazz band is the place for her?

Claire _____ others.

(4) Why is Claire nervous?

Claire is nervous because she will need to _____ with _____ _____ for a spot.

(5) When does Claire practice jazz songs?

Claire practices jazz songs _____ _____ with Lyle.

Do you play an instrument?

Who/What/When/Where/Why/How
A Different Kind of Plant

9

Level ★★

Score

Date   /   /

Name

/100

1 Read the following passage. Then answer the questions below using words from the passage.

10 points per question

Animals need food to live. The nutrients in food help them stay healthy. We know that some animals are meat eaters, but did you know that some plants are meat eaters, too? Most plants make their own food from the sun, but they get many of their nutrients from the soil. However, not all plants can get enough nutrients from the soil. These plants are meat eaters. They do not eat hamburger or chicken, although some do eat frogs! Mostly these plants get their nutrients from bugs. The Venus flytrap, for example, needs bugs for food.

Venus flytraps grow in soil that does not have enough nutrients to keep them healthy. They get nutrients by trapping bugs that live around them. Venus flytraps are native to bogs, or wet areas, in North Carolina and South Carolina, but their seeds have been planted in other places. Sometimes people keep them in their homes or in their gardens. There are not many Venus flytraps in the wild now, because there is less bog land now than there once was. This is one reason that these rare plants are endangered in the wild.

(1) What do plants that are meat eaters *NOT* eat?

They do not eat _____.

(2) How do Venus flytraps get their nutrients?

Venus flytraps get nutrients by _____ that live around them.

(3) Where are Venus flytraps native to?

Venus flytraps are native to bogs, or wet areas, _____

_____.

(4) What is one reason that there are not many Venus flytraps in the wild now?

One reason that there are not many Venus flytraps in the wild now is that there is _____ than there once was.

2 Read the following passage. Then answer the questions below using words from the passage.

10 points per question

During the spring, white flowers bloom on the Venus flytrap. But do not be fooled by these pretty flowers! The leaves that grow next to them are traps that catch flies and other bugs.

These leaves are like mouths. A bug flies or crawls onto the leaves to drink juice from them. The leaves have tiny hairs. A bug touches the hairs while drinking, which causes the leaf to close over the bug. The leaf closes very quickly, but it will not close all the way over a dead bug or something that does not move. Only a moving bug causes the leaf to close! After the bug is caught, it is covered in juices from the plant. Then the plant takes the nutrients from the bug.

Scientists are interested in how Venus flytraps move. They have studied the plants for a long time, but still do not have all the answers. Other people think Venus flytraps are interesting, too. People have taken Venus flytraps from their native bogs to sell or bring home. This has helped cause Venus flytraps to become endangered. There are now laws that protect Venus flytraps in the wild.

(1) What happens to the Venus flytrap during the spring?

During the spring, _____ on the Venus flytraps.

(2) Why does a bug fly onto the leaves of a Venus flytrap?

A bug flies onto the leaves _____.

(3) How does a Venus flytrap's leaf catch a bug?

A bug touches the hairs of the leaf _____, which causes the leaf

_____.

(4) When is a bug covered in juices from a Venus flytrap?

_____, it is covered in juices from a Venus flytrap.

(5) What does the Venus flytrap take from a bug?

The Venus flytrap takes the _____ from a bug.

(6) What has helped cause Venus flytraps to be endangered?

People have _____

_____, causing them to become endangered.

A plant that eats bugs! Cool!

© Kumon Publishing Co., Ltd. 19

Vocabulary Review

1 Pick the correct word from the box to complete each sentence below.

6 points per question

currency	locations	instrument	nervous	native

(1) When I have to speak in front of the class, I get _____.

(2) My favorite _____ is the trombone.

(3) Fast-food chains always have many _____.

(4) Zebras are _____ to Africa because they are originally from there.

(5) The American _____ is called the dollar.

2 Read the sentences. Then choose a word in bold from one of the sentences to match each definition below.

6 points per question

-- It was a matter of **historical** record that the town's name had been changed three times in the last thirty years.

-- The **mixture** we made in the kitchen tasted terrible.

-- The **designers** of the new car spent a long time thinking about the engine before looking at anything else.

-- After the crowd chased the monster to the **bog**, they lost it in among the reeds.

-- Charlie "The Bird" Parker is one of the most famous **saxophone** players of all time.

(1) _____   a product of combining or blending

(2) _____   a woodwind instrument

(3) _____   wet spongy ground

(4) _____   relating to a record of the past

(5) _____   people who create a plan for a project

Complete the crossword puzzle using the sentences below as clues. Use capital letters.

5 points per question

ACROSS

(1) A comedian's job is to ___?___ .

(2) The cheerleaders got everyone to ___?___ in a chant.

(3) My mother has a ring with my father's name ___?___ on it.

(4) The ___?___ to the math problem was very difficult.

DOWN

(5) Broccoli has lots of ___?___ in it, so it's good for you.

(6) ___?___ have found that most berries are healthy.

(7) The gorilla is an ___?___ animal. There aren't many left.

(8) I like the beat of this song, but not the ___?___ .

If you get stuck, try looking back a few pages. These words are from this section of the book!

True or False
Did You Know?

11

Level ★★

Score

Date   /   /

Name

/100

1 Complete the passage using the vocabulary words defined below.

4 points per question

Most houses used to be made of wood before stronger (1) _____ were invented. Now, because most houses are made using (2) _____ instead of wood, they last longer. A modern house is built on top of a stronger (3) _____ made with cement. Today, when we (4) _____ a house, it's more likely to last.

concrete	a mixture of cement with sand and gravel
construct	to put something together
materials	what a thing is made from
foundation	a strong base from which a building is built up

2 Read the passage. Then identify the statements below as **T** (true) or **F** (false) according to the passage.

6 points per question

Long ago, carpenters played a greater role in the construction of buildings because wood was one of the most readily available materials. When people started using steel and concrete, more types of craftspeople became necessary for construction.

Much like house construction, road construction has changed, too. Before the automobile was invented, roads in North America were often paths made by animals and people as they walked about. Today, road construction requires much planning and work to handle the large number of automobiles.

(1) Carpenters used to play a bigger role in building construction.   T   F

(2) Steel and concrete are used in building construction less often these days.   T   F

(3) Before cars, paths were made by people and animals.   T   F

(4) Building roads today takes much planning and work.   T   F

(5) House and road construction has not changed over the years.   T   F

3 Read the passage. Then identify the statements below as **T** (true) or **F** (false) according to the passage.

8 points per question

The Panama Canal is a human-made waterway that allows ships to cross a narrow strip of land in Panama. Before the canal was built, ships traveling from the Atlantic to the Pacific Ocean had to travel around South America. After the canal was opened, ships could cross through Panama and save a lot of time.

The canal was difficult to construct. Several countries tried and failed before the United States succeeded in 1914. A big problem was that mosquitoes spread many diseases. Earlier, France gave up on the project after thousands of workers lost their lives.

(1) The Panama Canal is a natural waterway.　　　　　**T**　　**F**

(2) Before the canal, traveling from the Atlantic to the Pacific　　**T**　　**F**
Ocean took a lot more time.

(3) Construction of the canal was easy.　　　　　　**T**　　**F**

(4) Many people died while working on the canal.　　　**T**　　**F**

4 Read the passage and complete the statement using words from the passage only.

11 points per question

The Panama Canal has been very successful. This shortcut saves ships thousands of miles of travel. Before the canal was constructed, ships made a 13,000 mile journey from New York to San Francisco. However, after the canal was built, the trip was shortened to 5,200 miles.

Every day over 30 ships pass through the canal. The waterway saves time and money, but ships have to pay a heavy toll. On May 30th, 2006, a ship established a new toll record by paying $249,165. Richard Halliburton paid the lowest toll to date when he swam across the Panama Canal in 1928. He paid only 36 cents!

(1) After the canal was built, the journey from New York to San Francisco was

_____.

(2) The canal saves ships time, but they have

to _____.

Canal construction is complicated!

True or False
Soccer Over the Years

12

Level ★★

Score

/100

Date   /   /

Name

1 Complete the passage using the vocabulary words defined below.

4 points per question

People in almost every country enjoy the game of soccer either as players or by going to the games as (1) _____. The rules are almost the same worldwide. The object is to score points against your (2) _____ by kicking or heading the ball into their net. Players can (3) _____ the ball with their feet, or pass it to a (4) _____.

dribble	to move a soccer ball along with short kicks
teammate(s)	fellow member of a team
opponent(s)	someone who is on the other team in a sport
spectator(s)	people who watch without taking part

2 Read the passage. Then identify the statements below as **T** (true) or **F** (false) according to the passage.

6 points per question

Soccer players have to be fit because they may run as many as six or seven miles during a game. While running, the player with the ball must kick, head, or dribble it downfield. The goalies are the sole players that can touch the ball with their hands.

Perhaps the greatest soccer player was Pele. A native of Brazil, Pele led his country to three World Cup wins in twelve years. He retired as a player in 1977.

(1) Soccer players do not run very much.   T   F

(2) Soccer players can hit the ball with their head.   T   F

(3) The goalies cannot touch the ball with their hands.   T   F

(4) Brazil won three World Cups with Pele on their team.   T   F

3 Read the passage. Then identify the statements below as **T** (true) or **F** (false) according to the passage.

8 points per question

Children grow up playing soccer in Europe, Asia, and South America, and crowds of over 150,000 attend important soccer matches. The sport is a source of national pride, and these parts of the world take soccer very seriously.

One of the reasons soccer is so popular is that the basic rules are very simple. Both players and spectators alike can easily understand them. Also, the things you need to play soccer — a ball and a field — can be found almost anywhere. Even in poorer countries, people can find some type of soccer ball and the space to play.

Even though a ball is all you really need, balls have changed over the years. Early soccer balls were stuffed with rags and hair. Other balls were hard and about the size of a softball. A rubber ball similar to the kind used today was invented in 1855.

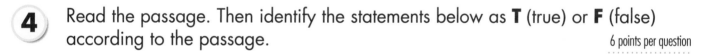

(1)   Crowds of over 150,000 attend some soccer matches in Europe.　　**T**　　**F**

(2)   Soccer is important to national pride in many countries.　　**T**　　**F**

(3)   The basic rules in soccer are difficult to understand.　　**T**　　**F**

(4)   You can play soccer with only a ball and a field.　　**T**　　**F**

(5)   Soccer balls have stayed the same over the years.　　**T**　　**F**

(6)   Soccer balls are stuffed with hair today.　　**T**　　**F**

4 Read the passage. Then identify the statements below as **T** (true) or **F** (false) according to the passage.

6 points per question

People disagree on which country was the first to play soccer. Some say it was China because they played a soccer — like game over 3,000 years ago. Others say it was Italy because the Romans played a game more similar to today's soccer.

(1)   The Chinese played a game like soccer 3,000 years ago.　　**T**　　**F**

(2)   The Romans played a game less similar to today's soccer　　**T**　　**F**
　　　　than the ancient Chinese did.

Do you like soccer? I do!

True or False
Gorilla Surprises

Level ★ ★

Score

Date   /   /

Name

/100

1 Complete the passage using the vocabulary words defined below.

4 points per question

Many animals that are normally (1) _____ sometimes have to behave differently in order to (2) _____ in the wild. If an (3) _____ comes into the personal space of an animal, it has to (4) _____ its space and family.

survive	to continue to live
peaceful	without violence or disagreement
defend	to protect
intruder	an unwelcome person/animal

2 Read the passage. Then identify the statements below as **T** (true) or **F** (false) according to the passage.

5 points per question

The gorilla is the largest of the apes and lives in the rain forests of Africa. Gorillas look very fierce with their large, shiny faces and strong teeth. In truth, they are usually calm and peaceful unless attacked or disturbed. Their hair is black or brown and covers most of their body except for the chest, the face, the palms of their hands, and the soles of their feet. When a gorilla is upset or wants to scare off intruders, it stands on its legs and beats its chest.

(1) The largest of all animals is the gorilla.   T   F

(2) Africa has no rain forests.   T   F

(3) Gorillas are not usually fierce and dangerous.   T   F

(4) Gorillas are calm even when disturbed.   T   F

(5) A gorilla's chest is covered with very thick hair.   T   F

(6) Gorillas sometimes try to scare off intruders.   T   F

3 Read the passage. Then identify the statements below as **T** (true) or **F** (false) according to the passage.

7 points per question

> Gorillas lead a fairly simple and peaceful life. They move about the forests of Africa in groups of up to thirty. A group might be made up of one or two males, a few females, and the children.
>
> A male is always the head of the group. This leader decides where the group should go, when they should get up, and when they should rest. Most importantly, this male defends the group from danger.

(1)   The life of a gorilla is fairly peaceful.   **T**   **F**

(2)   Gorillas move about in groups of up to thirty.   **T**   **F**

(3)   A group is made up of only males.   **T**   **F**

(4)   The head of a group is male.   **T**   **F**

(5)   The female gorilla makes the decisions.   **T**   **F**

(6)   The leader protects his group from danger.   **T**   **F**

4 Read the passage and complete the statement using words from the passage only.

6 points per question

> Some gorillas in zoos have lived to be 50 years old. It is hard to know, however, how long they live in the jungle. Most gorillas probably do not live to be as old as 50 in the wild because they suffer from many diseases.
>
> It is sad to know that the only real enemy of the gorilla is humankind. People have hunted these animals for food and destroyed their forest homes. As a result, gorillas are now endangered in many areas where they were once plentiful.

(1)   Gorillas in the jungle probably do not survive as long as those _____.

(2)   Humankind is the _____ of the gorilla.

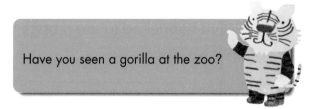

Have you seen a gorilla at the zoo?

Date   /   /

Name

1 Read the passage. Then answer the questions using words from the passage.

10 points per question

Once upon a time, a large group of elephants lived in the jungle. The King was a huge, majestic elephant with large tusks, and he looked after the other elephants with care.

One year, there was a bad drought, and it did not rain for weeks and weeks. Many birds and animals died of thirst.

The King knew that if he did not get water for his herd soon, many elephants would die, too.

He asked all the elephants to spread out in the jungle and look for water. The elephants went as quickly as they could.

One elephant found a beautiful lake full of water. The King was happy and ordered all the elephants to follow him to the lake. All of the elephants thirstily ran behind the King to the new lake.

Near the lake was a colony of rabbits. When the elephants came through their colony, they scared many rabbits and destroyed many houses.

(1) Why were birds and animals dying of thirst?

There was a bad _____ and it _____ for weeks and weeks.

(2) What would happen if the King did not get water for his herd soon?

If the King did not get water for his herd soon, many elephants _____.

(3) How did the King try to solve the situation?

The King asked all the elephants to _____ in the jungle and

_____.

(4) What happened to the rabbits when the elephants went to the lake?

The elephants _____ and _____

_____.

2 Read the passage. Then number the statements below in the order in which they occurred in the passage. *60 points for completion*

The King of Rabbits called a meeting. "A herd of elephants has moved to our lake. When they travel, they scare us and destroy our homes. We have to take urgent steps to save ourselves, so I want all of you to think of a way to stop the elephants."

One little rabbit raised his paw.

"Your Majesty, if you will send me to the elephants as your messenger, I might be able to save us."

The King of Rabbits sent the little rabbit to the elephants that night. The little rabbit climbed a rock and called for the King of Elephants.

"Well, who are you?" asked the King of Elephants.

"I am a messenger," said the little rabbit. "I am a messenger from the mighty Moon."

"What is your business?" said the elephant, while drawing closer to the tiny rabbit. The rabbit got scared.

"I have a message for you. Please try not to be angry with me, for a messenger should not be punished for his message. He is only doing his duty."

"Very well," agreed the King, "I will not harm you. Say what you have come to say."

"The Moon has commanded me to tell you, the King of the Elephants, that you have brought your herd to the Moon's holy lake and soiled its waters."

(   ) ⓐ   The King of Elephants agreed not to harm the rabbit.

(1) ⓑ   The King of Rabbits asked everyone to think of a solution.

(   ) ⓒ   The little rabbit asked the King of Elephants not to hurt him.

(   ) ⓓ   The little rabbit told the King of Elephants that the elephants had soiled the Moon's holy lake.

(   ) ⓔ   The little rabbit climbed a rock and called for the King of Elephants.

(   ) ⓕ   The little rabbit told the King of Elephants that he was a messenger for the Moon.

(   ) ⓖ   The little rabbit raised his paw.

What a brave rabbit!

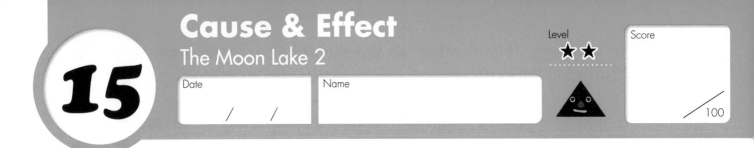

Cause & Effect
The Moon Lake 2

Level
★ ★

Date
/ /

Name

Score
/ 100

15

1 Read the passage. Then answer the questions using words from the passage.

10 points per question

The rabbit paused, and could see the King of Elephants was shocked. Even though the rabbit was scared, he continued.

"You know that rabbits are under the Moon's protection, don't you? Everyone knows that the King of Rabbits is friends with the Moon. I ask you only not to scare any more rabbits. If you do not obey what I say, terrible things will happen to your herd."

At first the King of Elephants was speechless. He thought for a while and then spoke.

"You are correct. We may have scared many rabbits on the way to this lake. I was only trying to provide for my herd. I would like to make sure you do not suffer anymore, and I would like to apologize to the Moon. Please tell me what to do."

"Come with me alone," said the little rabbit, "and I will take you to the Moon."

The little rabbit took the King of Elephants to the lake, where they saw the Moon reflected in the still waters.

"Please meet the Moon, your majesty," said the little rabbit.

(1) What was the first message the rabbit had from the Moon?

The rabbit said that rabbits are _____.

(2) What does the little rabbit say will happen to the herd if the King of Elephants does not obey the Moon?

If the King does not heed what the Moon said, _____ will

_____ the herd.

(3) What was the result of the rabbit's speech?

At first, the King of Elephants _____ but then he _____

for a while and _____.

(4) What two things would the King of Elephants like to do?

The King would like to _____ the rabbits do not _____,

and he would like to _____ to the Moon.

2 Read the passage. Then answer the questions below.

"I want to apologize to the Moon," said the King of Elephants. He dipped his trunk into the lake. The water was disturbed, and he sent ripples through the lake. The Moon seemed to wobble and the rabbit got angry.

"Now the Moon is angrier than ever!" said the rabbit.

"What have I done? Why is it angry?" said the King of Elephants.

"You have disturbed the waters of the Moon's lake," replied the rabbit.

The King of Elephants bowed his head in sorrow.

"Please ask the Moon to forgive me. We will never touch the water of this lake again. We will never harm the rabbits that the Moon loves so dearly," said the King of Elephants.

He led his herd carefully away from the lake, and the rabbits rejoiced. The lake was once again safe. A short time later, the rains returned to the jungle and all the animals were happy.

(1) Why did the King of Elephants touch the lake?

    ⓐ He was thirsty.

    ⓑ He was trying to apologize to the Moon.

    ⓒ He wanted to see the ripples in the water.   (   )

(2) According to the rabbit, what caused the Moon to be angrier than ever?

    ⓐ The King of Elephants harmed a rabbit.

    ⓑ The King of Elephants wanted to say hello to the Moon.

    ⓒ The King of Elephants disturbed the waters of the lake.   (   )

(3) What effect did the Moon's anger have on the King of Elephants?

    ⓐ He led his herd carefully away from the lake.

    ⓑ He drank more water.

    ⓒ He begged for rain.   (   )

A little thinking can always overcome a big problem!

16

Level
★ ★

Score
/100

Date   /   /   Name

1 Read the passage. Then answer the questions below.

24 points per question

Blake hated science class. The teacher always called on him, and he often didn't know the answers. Also, he thought a lot of the things they learned about were disgusting. He didn't want to know about the insides of animals.

Probably because he didn't like science class, Blake kept putting off the big science project for that year. He just didn't feel like doing it.

Suddenly, the project was due the next day, and he had to come up with something. He was sitting on the back porch after dinnner and staring at the ants when he had an idea.

"What kinds of food do ants like best?" he thought.

That seemed like an easy idea, so he started by finding an old fishbowl in the basement. He gathered some ants and some dirt and put them in the bowl. Then he put some cheese, some sugar, a half of a tomato, and a piece of bread in the bowl with the ants. It all took a long time, so Blake took the bowl into the kitchen, covered it with a board, and went to bed.

(1) Why did Blake not like science class? Put a check (✓) next to all the reasons that appear in the passage.

( ) ⓐ The teacher always called on him.

( ) ⓑ He would rather be outside.

( ) ⓒ He didn't know the answers.

( ) ⓓ The topics were disgusting.

( ) ⓔ He didn't like the teacher.

(2) What were the reasons Blake decided to do a project about ants? Put a check (✓) next to all the reasons that appear in the passage.

( ) ⓐ The project was due the next day.

( ) ⓑ He liked ants.

( ) ⓒ It was an easy project.

2 Read the passage. Then answer the questions below.

The next morning, Blake woke up to a shriek. He ran downstairs to see what had happened.

His mother was standing in the middle of the kitchen, which was full of ants. She looked at him with a frown.

"Did you have something to do with this?" she asked.

"I'm so sorry, Mom! This is my science project. I guess the ants found a way out of the fishbowl," Blake replied.

They inspected the cover on the fishbowl and found that the ants had eaten through the wood he put on top of the bowl.

"Blake, these aren't ants," his mother said. "They are termites!"

Blake was embarrassed, but he had to help clean up as fast as he could. He still had to get to school and figure out what to do for his science project. His mother left the room, so he decided his punishment was to clean up.

Blake swept up as many of the termites as he could find on the floor. He wiped them off the counters, the corners, and he even found some on the ceiling! He cleaned as quickly and as completely as he could. He didn't want the termites eating the wood in their house.

Just as he was about to throw out the dirt and food left in the bowl, his mother came back in. She was carrying a bag.

"Blake, I got you some real ants outside. Next time, try to plan your project a little earlier, will you?" his mother said with a little smile.

(1) Number the statements below in the order in which they occurred in the passage.

32 points for completion

( ) ⓐ Blake woke up to a shriek.

( ) ⓑ Blake's mother found him some real ants.

( ) ⓒ Blake and his mother inspected the wood and found that the termites had eaten through it.

( ) ⓓ Blake cleaned up the termites.

(2) What did Blake learn as a result of his experience with his science project? 20 points

Blake learned that next time, he should try to _____ his

_____.

It always pays to plan ahead!

Vocabulary Review

Date   /   /   Name

1 Pick the correct word from the box to complete each sentence below.

6 points per question

| concrete | dribble | intruder | apologized | protection |

(1) When the alarm went off, we thought there was an _____ in the house, but it was just our cat.

(2) Jim can't pass that well, but he can really _____!

(3) Buildings made out of _____ last long.

(4) Shin pads provide good _____ when you play soccer.

(5) I _____ for trampling Dad's tomato vine in the back yard.

2 Read the sentences. Then choose a word in bold from one of the sentences to match each definition below.

6 points per question

-- The dinner I made was **terrible** but everyone was happy I tried.

-- The mountain was **majestic** as it rose high above the town.

-- Charlotte's dog has a **fierce** snarl, but it's actually very nice.

-- Learning how to make fire is an important skill if you want to **survive** in the wild.

-- Mrs. Sandovsky left an **urgent** message for the director.

(1) _____ having or exhibiting greatness

(2) _____ violently hostile or aggressive

(3) _____ to remain alive

(4) _____ calling for immediate attention

(5) _____ extremely bad

3 Complete the crossword puzzle using the sentences below as clues.
Use capital letters.

5 points per question

Crossword grid with clue numbers: (7), (5), (6), (1), (2), (8), (3), (4)

Pre-filled letters visible in grid:
(5) O, (2) S P, (6) T, (1) I S, C, (8) M, M, (3) P, C, T, (4) S, L

ACROSS

(1) The detective had to ___?___ the evidence quickly.

(2) Sometimes the ___?___ can get very loud at sporting events.

(3) It's so ___?___ out here in the middle of this lake.

(4) Folding paper planes is ___?___ once you know how.

DOWN

(5) My favorite team was struggling against its ___?___ all game.

(6) One ___?___ of ours always brings orange slices to practice.

(7) Lester's nap was ___?___ by the sound of a dog barking.

(8) This jacket is made from a smooth ___?___.

You know your words!

18

Main Idea
Traveling

Level ★★

Score

/ 100

Date   /   /

Name

1 Read the passage. Then answer the questions below.

In the morning, Wen waits for the school bus. Wen has lots of friends to sit with on the bus. But not everyone Wen knows takes the bus to school. People who do not live on the bus route use different kinds of transportation. No matter how they travel to school, all of Wen's friends get there.

Wen's friend Freddy lives only a few blocks from school. Freddy walks to school, even when it rains. Freddy's older sister goes to school in the city. She takes a bus to the city, and then she takes a train to school. She has to buy a ticket for the bus and a card for the train.

Wen's friend Peter lives too close to school to use the bus. But he lives too far from school to walk there. Peter's mother drives him to school in the morning. Sometimes they carpool with other classmates and their parents. Carpooling with other families lets Peter's mom spend less time driving. She and the other parents also save money on the gas that their cars use as fuel. Peter likes when they carpool because he can talk to his friends on the way to school.

(1) Use the choices in the box on the right to fill in the chart below.   10 points per question

Person	Way of travel
Wen	① school bus
Freddy	②
Freddy's sister	③
Peter	④

car

bus and train

school bus

walking

(2) What could be a good title for this passage? Choose an answer from the box.   20 points

Title:
School bus
Walking
Train and bus
Car and carpooling

ⓐ The School Bus

ⓑ How Students Go to School

ⓒ Carpooling

ⓓ Saving Money on Fuel

2 Read the passage. Then answer the questions below.

20 points per question

Wen's teacher, Mrs. Patel, does not walk, ride a bus, or a drive a car to school. She rides her bike to school almost every day. Biking is her favorite kind of transportation. She likes it more than taking a train or driving her car.

Mrs. Patel says riding her bike is not just a way to go places. Riding her bike is fun, so she does it as much as she can! Sometimes she even rides her bike to the grocery store. She puts the food she buys in the bike's basket. Mrs. Patel likes the exercise that she gets from riding her bike. Last fall, Mrs. Patel was in a bike race. She had to train very hard, but she thought the training was fun.

Mrs. Patel says that riding her bike is also good for the planet. Riding a bike to school saves fuel. Her car needs gas fuel to run, but it is important not to waste fuel. Her car also puts poisons in the air, but her bike doesn't! Her bike does not need gas because its fuel is pedal power. That means she makes the bike move by pedaling!

(1) What could be a good title for this passage? Choose an answer from the box.

Title:
Biking is her favorite kind of transportation.
She bikes as much as she can.
She likes to exercise by riding her bike.
She likes that riding her bike is good for the planet.

ⓐ Mrs. Patel: Bike Rider
ⓑ The Bike Race
ⓒ Saving Fuel
ⓓ The Long Ride

┌─ **Don't forget!** ─────────────────────────────

The **main idea** is a statement that expresses the most important information in a passage or paragraph.

For example, the main idea of the second paragraph above is:
Mrs. Patel thinks riding her bike is fun, so she does it as much as she can!

└──

(2) What is the main idea of the paragraph in gray? Put a check (✓) next to the correct idea below.

(   ) ⓐ Mrs. Patel's car needs fuel to run.

(   ) ⓑ Riding a bike is fun.

(   ) ⓒ Riding a bike to school is good for the planet.

Do you like riding your bike?

Main Idea
Flags of the World

19

Level ★★

Date / /

Name

Score

/100

1 Read the passage. Then answer the questions below.

Every country in the world has a flag. A flag is a piece of fabric with a picture or pattern on it. The flag is a symbol that stands for the country. It is a custom in many places for people to fly, or hang, a flag. The flag tells something about the country and its culture. This may be about its land, its history, or the things that the people do there.

Many flags have patterns of stripes. The flag of Italy has a green stripe, a white stripe, and a red stripe. Each stripe tells something about Italy. The white stripe is a symbol of Italy's snowy mountains. The flag of Chad also has three stripes. They are blue, red, and orange. Some flags show pictures. The flag of Canada has a picture of a red maple leaf, which is a symbol of the maple trees in Canada. The Mexican flag has both a pattern of stripes and a picture. The picture shows an eagle eating a snake. This picture comes from a very old Mexican story.

A flag may also tell about a country's past. The American flag is called the Stars and Stripes. It has a pattern of fifty stars and thirteen stripes. The fifty stars are a symbol of the fifty states in the country, and the thirteen stripes are a symbol of the country's first thirteen colonies.

(1) Use the information given in the passage to fill in the chart below.

10 points per question

Description of Flag	Country
Green, white, and red stripes	①
Shows a maple leaf	②
Blue, red and orange stripes	③
Stars and Stripes	④
Shows an eagle eating a snake	⑤

(2) What is a good title for the whole passage? Put a check (✓) next to the correct title below.

10 points

( ) ⓐ A Flag for Every Country

( ) ⓑ The Stars and Stripes

( ) ⓒ How to Fly a Flag

2 Read the passage. Then answer the questions below.

Many places have their own flag. Did you know that there is a flag for every state in the United States? There is even a flag for the planet Mars! But a flag can be more than a symbol for a place.

A flag may be a symbol of a group, a school, or an event like the Olympics. The flag of the Olympics shows five rings of different colors that connect. Each ring is a symbol for a part of the world that joins in the Olympics. The Red Cross is a group that helps people who are in trouble. If a person sees the Red Cross flag, which has a red cross against a white background, he knows he can ask for help. People may fly a flag as a custom on a holiday. Children's Day in Japan is a holiday when the country wishes for children's happiness. It is a custom on this day to fly a flag with a picture of a fish.

Flags are used as a way to talk. A flag with patterns can be very helpful to people who do not speak the same language. Sailors on ships use flags to talk to sailors on other ships. They may not speak the same language, but they know what the patterns mean. A flag with blue and white squares says "no." A flag with five stripes that are blue, white, and red says "yes."

(1) Fill in the chart below using information from the second paragraph in the passage.

10 points per question

Flag	What Flag Means
①	Each ring is a symbol for each part of the world
Red Cross	Help for people who are in ② _____
Children's Day	A day to wish for ③ _____

(2) What is the main idea of the paragraph in gray? Put a check (✓) next to the correct idea below.

10 points

(   ) ⓐ A flag with blue and white squares says "no."

(   ) ⓑ Flags with patterns can be very helpful.

(   ) ⓒ Flags are used as a way to talk.

(   ) ⓓ Sailors know what the patterns mean.

What is your favorite flag?

Main Idea
Loving the Library

20

Level ★★

Date / /

Name

Score /100

1 Read the passage. Then answer the questions below.

10 points per question

Gina's favorite place was her town's library. She liked the library because it had something for everyone in her community. Everyone in town could find something to do at the library. When Gina was little, she used to go to the library to hear the librarian, Mr. Kim, read stories. But when she got older, she went for other reasons.

Most of the time, Gina went to the library to read books about frogs. Last month, she went to the library because she was curious about something. She asked Mr. Kim how she could find out if all frogs are green. He showed her how to look on the computer to find books in the library about frogs. She learned that not all frogs are green. After that, she wanted to read only about frogs.

Sometimes Gina checked out books about frogs and took them home with her. Some of the books were about what frogs eat and where they live. Some were stories about frogs. Gina was worried that soon she would have read all of the library's books about frogs. She had already read *A Frog Is a Friend* ten times. Mr. Kim told her that she could read articles in magazines about frogs, too. Gina thought she might try that, but today she came to the library for another reason. "Mr. Kim," she said, "how would I find out if all lions are yellow?"

(1) Think about the title in bold below. For which paragraph would it be a good title? Put a check (✓) next to the correct paragraph.

( ) ⓐ The first paragraph

Gina's Favorite Place

( ) ⓑ The second paragraph

( ) ⓒ The third paragraph

(2) What is the main idea of the paragraph in gray? Write the letter of the correct idea in the space below.

ⓐ Gina wanted to read only about frogs.

ⓑ Gina learned that not all frogs are green.

ⓒ Gina went on the computer.

( )

(3) What did Gina want to find out after she found out about frogs? Gina wanted to find out if _____.

2 Read the passage. Then answer the questions below.

The library really does have something for everyone in the community. Gina's library has a big comic book section. Gina's neighbor Justin goes to the library to read comic books. Justin never checks out the books he picks. Instead, he reads them on a bench at the library. Today, he waved at Gina, who was sitting at the table reading *A Lion Is Loud*. Justin sat quietly and read *Captain Max*.

Gina's dentist, Dr. Bell, also goes to the library. She goes to the library to read articles about teeth. She thinks that there is always something new to learn about teeth. Today she sat in the back of the library near the science magazines. She read an article called "Teeth Today." Dr. Bell thought it was a very interesting article.

Gina's friend Hayes goes to the library, too. Hayes does not go the library for just one thing. Hayes likes to do many things at the library. Sometimes he uses the Internet to do research for school projects. Sometimes he goes to hear authors talk about their books. Once he came to the library to see the library's new mural. The mural was a large picture that many members of the community had painted. But today Hayes came to read. He read a book about baseball called *The Fastball Book*. He could not put it down!

(1) What is the main idea of the paragraph in gray? Put a check (✓) next to the correct idea below.   20 points

    (   ) ⓐ Hayes does many things at the library.

    (   ) ⓑ Hayes uses the Internet at the library.

    (   ) ⓒ Many people in town painted a mural.

(2) What is a good title for the whole passage? Put a check (✓) next to the best title below.   20 points

    (   ) ⓐ Books at the Library

    (   ) ⓑ Something for Everyone at the Library

    (   ) ⓒ The Comic Book Section

(3) What did the people in Gina's community read today? Fill in the chart below using information from the passage.   10 points per question

Name of Person	What Person Read
Gina	A Lion is Loud
Justin	①
②	"Teeth Today"
Hayes	③

What do you read at the library?

Main Idea
The Golden Gate Bridge

21

Level ★★

Date / /

Name

Score / 100

1 Read the passage. Then answer the questions below.

15 points per question

The Golden Gate Bridge in California connects the city of San Francisco to Marin County. The Golden Gate Bridge is an amazing bridge. It spans, or stretches, almost two miles, and its deck weighs more than 150 thousand tons. But the Golden Gate Bridge is not just big. It is one of the most beautiful bridges in the world! The architects who designed it knew they were making something special. There had never been a bridge like it before.

Construction on the Golden Gate Bridge was finished in 1937. At the time, it was the longest suspension bridge in the world. A suspension bridge is a special kind of bridge that can span a long distance. Suspension bridges allow vehicles to make trips across water much faster. A suspension bridge is held up by two towers that are built on land or in shallow water. One of the Golden Gate Bridge's towers was built in the Pacific Ocean!

There are now other suspension bridges that are longer than the Golden Gate Bridge. One of them is in New York City. The longest suspension bridge in the world is in Japan. But the Golden Gate Bridge is still one of the longest and most famous suspension bridges.

(1) What is the main idea of the paragraph in gray? Put a check (✓) next to the correct idea below.

(　) ⓐ The Golden Gate Bridge is one of the most beautiful bridges in the world.

(　) ⓑ The Golden Gate Bridge is the longest bridge in the world.

(　) ⓒ The Golden Gate Bridge is a suspension bridge.

(2) Fill in the chart for the paragraph in gray using the correct phrases in the box.

Suspension Bridges

Can span a long distance
Deck Weighs 150 thousand tons
Have two towers
Stretches almost three miles
Make travel faster
One tower built in Pacific Ocean

2 Read the passage. Then answer the questions below.

Building the Golden Gate Bridge took a lot of labor. Construction of the bridge lasted four years and cost thirty-five million dollars. That cost today would be over one billion dollars! The workers built the bridge with concrete and steel. To build one of the bridge's towers, they had to labor 100 feet below the sea!

The architects who designed the Golden Gate Bridge wanted it to be beautiful to look at. But they knew that the bridge needed to be strong to be safe. They had to plan very carefully. The towers that hold the bridge up needed to be very strong because the bridge is so heavy. Because San Francisco has earthquakes, the towers also needed to be sturdy enough to remain standing during such an event. The bridge was also designed to sway in the ocean winds. Swaying is safer for the bridge than if it stood still in the wind. The bridge can sway 27 feet!

When they planned the bridge, the architects thought about how the bridge would look, too. The Golden Gate Bridge is not really golden. That name comes from the water underneath the bridge. The bridge is painted an orange color (known as international orange), which makes the bridge beautiful. This color was chosen for another reason, too. It makes the bridge easy to see, which helps stop ship accidents.

(1) What is the best title for the second paragraph of the passage? 10 points

    ⓐ A Beautiful Bridge

    ⓑ Planning the Golden Gate Bridge

    ⓒ 100 Feet Below the Sea   (   )

(2) What is the main idea of the entire passage? 10 points

    ⓐ Building the Golden Gate Bridge was a lot of work.

    ⓑ The bridge needed to be strong to be safe.

    ⓒ The Golden Gate Bridge is not really golden.   (   )

(3) Complete the chart below to show why the architects made the choices they did.

10 points per question

Architect's plan	Reason for architect's plan
Towers are very strong	bridge is ① _____ San Francisco has ② _____
Bridge can ③ _____	ocean winds
Bridge is ④ _____	beautiful ⑤ _____ to see

Do you have a favorite bridge?

22 Vocabulary Review

1 Pick the correct word from the box to complete each sentence below.

6 points per question

pattern	ripples	span	cultures	fuel

(1) One _____ of the bridge was painted green to honor Earth Day.

(2) Our van runs on a special _____, not gas.

(3) We made my red dress out of a _____ I designed!

(4) Dogs are considered dirty in some _____.

(5) When the lake is still, you can see the _____ made by the bugs when they touch the water.

2 Read the sentences. Then choose a word in bold from one of the sentences to match each definition below.

6 points per question

-- The **architect** said that the tower was too tall.

-- It is a **custom** among some island cultures to place a hot object on the forehead of a sick child.

-- The chemicals from the factory were a **poison** to the plants around it.

-- The **suspension** bridge swayed in the heavy winds.

-- Our fourth-grade class painted a **mural** on the side of the gym.

(1) _____ a practice common to a people or place

(2) _____ the state of being hung

(3) _____ a work of art applied to a wall

(4) _____ one who plans buildings

(5) _____ something destructive or harmful

3 Complete the crossword puzzle using the sentences below as clues. Use capital letters.

5 points per question

(5)

		(6)		(7)		(8)	
				C		C	
(1) T	R		O		T		
						M	
Q			T		O		
(2) L	B						
			C	(3) A		C	
(4)	Y		O				

ACROSS

(1) My favorite method of ___?___ is the train.

(2) The doghouse was small but required hours of ___?___.

(3) Today, there was an ___?___ in the newspaper about my school!

(4) The stripes on the American flag are a ___?___ of the original colonies.

DOWN

(5) ___?___ cause damage to buildings when the ground shakes.

(6) Our bus to school was delayed by ___?___ work on the highway.

(7) There are three other children that are in my ___?___ to school.

(8) My whole ___?___ got together for a festival at the park.

You got it!

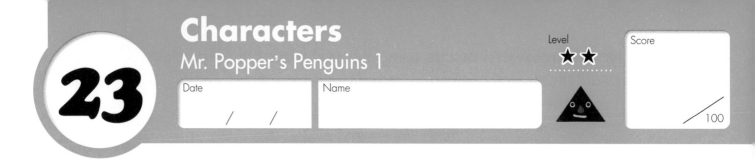

Characters
Mr. Popper's Penguins 1

Level ★★

Date / /

Name

Score /100

1 Read the passage from *Mr. Popper's Penguins* by Florence Atwater. Then answer the questions below using words from the passage.

10 points per question

> It was an afternoon in late September. In the pleasant little city of Stillwater, Mr. Popper, the house painter, was going home from work.
>
> He was carrying his buckets, his ladders, and his boards so that he had rather a hard time moving along. He was spattered here and there with paint and calcimine*, and there were bits of wallpaper clinging to his hair and whiskers, for he was rather an untidy man.
>
> The children looked up from their play to smile at him as he passed, and the housewives, seeing him, said "Oh dear, there goes Mr. Popper. I must remember to ask John to have the house painted over in the spring."
>
> No one knew what went on inside of Mr. Popper's head, and no one guessed that he would one day be the most famous person in Stillwater.

calcimine – glue and water mix used to put up plaster

(1) When and where does this story start?

This story starts in _____ in the pleasant _____

_____ .

(2) What did the housewives think when they saw Mr. Popper pass by?

The housewives thought they should ask their husbands to have their houses

_____ .

(3) What is the surprising fact about Mr. Popper?

Surprisingly, Mr. Popper would _____

_____ .

(4) What is the main idea of the paragraph in gray?

Mr. Popper was rather _____ .

2

Read the passage. Then identify the statements below as **T** (true) or **F** (false) according to the passage.

10 points per question

He was a dreamer. Even when he was busiest smoothing down the paste on the wallpaper, or painting the outside of other people's houses, he would forget what he was doing. Once he had painted three sides of a kitchen green, and the other side yellow. …

The reason that Mr. Popper was so absent-minded was that he was always dreaming about far-away countries. He had never been out of Stillwater. Not that he was unhappy. He had a nice little house of his own, a wife whom he loved dearly, and two children, named Janie and Bill. Still, it would have been nice, he often thought, if he could have seen something of the world before he met Mrs. Popper and settled down. He had never hunted tigers in India, or climbed the peaks of the Himalayas, or dived for pearls in the South Seas. Above all, he had never seen the Poles.

That was what he regretted most of all. He had never seen those great shining white expanses of ice and snow. How he wished that he had been a scientist, instead of a house painter in Stillwater, so that he might have joined some of the great Polar expeditions. Since he could not go, he was always thinking about them.

(1)　Mr. Popper often forgot what he was doing.　　　　　**T**　　**F**

(2)　Mr. Popper had traveled far and wide.　　　　　**T**　　**F**

(3)　Mr. Popper was unhappy.　　　　　**T**　　**F**

(4)　Mr. Popper was a great hunter.　　　　　**T**　　**F**

(5)　Mr. Popper wants to go to the Poles most of all.　　　　　**T**　　**F**

(6)　Mr. Popper would rather have been a scientist.　　　　　**T**　　**F**

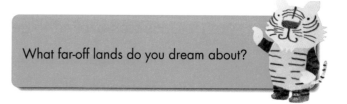

What far-off lands do you dream about?

Level
★★★

Date
/   /

Name

Score
/100

1 Read the passage. Then answer the questions below by putting a check (✓) next to all of the correct statements.

20 points per question

* Here, we pick up the story of Mr. Popper just a few pages later.

The bell rang again, a little louder this time. Grumbling to himself, Mr. Popper went to the door.

It was not the postman who stood there. It was an expressman with the largest box Mr. Popper had ever seen.

"Party by the name of Popper live here?"

"That's me."

"Well, here's a package that's come Air Express all the way from Antarctica. Some journey, I'll say."

Mr. Popper signed the receipt and examined the box. It was covered all over with markings. "UNPACK AT ONCE," said one. "KEEP COOL," said another. He noticed that the box was punched here and there with air holes.

You can imagine that once he had the box inside the house, Mr. Popper wasted no time in getting the screw driver, for by this time, of course, he had guessed it was the surprise from Admiral Drake.

He had succeeded in removing the outer boards and part of the packing, which was a layer of dry ice, when from the depths of the packing case he suddenly heard a faint "*Ork.*" His heart stood still. Surely he had heard that sound before at the Drake Expedition movies. His hands were trembling so that he could scarcely lift off the last of the wrappings.

(1) What did Mr. Popper know about the package? You may select more than one answer.

( ) ⓐ The package came from Antarctica.

( ) ⓑ The package was very large.

( ) ⓒ The package was the surprise from Admiral Drake.

( ) ⓓ The package was moving.

(2) Why were Mr. Popper's hands trembling? You may select more than one answer.

( ) ⓐ He was excited to get the package.

( ) ⓑ He thought he knew what was inside the package.

( ) ⓒ He was afraid.

2 Read the passage. Then answer the questions below.

There was not the slightest doubt about it. It was a penguin.

Mr. Popper was speechless with delight.

But the penguin was not speechless. "*Ork,*" it said again, but this time it held out its flippers and jumped over the packing debris.

It was a stout little fellow about two and a half feet high. Although it was about the size of a small child, it looked much more like a little gentleman, with its smooth white waistcoat in front and its long black tailcoat dragging a little behind. Its eyes were set in two white circles in its black head. It turned its head from one side to the other, as first with one eye, and then with the other, it examined Mr. Popper.

Mr. Popper had read that penguins are extremely curious, and he soon found out that this was true, for stepping out, the visitor began to inspect the house. Down the hall it went and into the bedrooms, with its strange, pompous little strut. When it, or he — Mr. Popper began to think of it as a he — got to the bathroom, it looked around with a pleased expression on its face.

"Perhaps," thought Mr. Popper, "all that white tiling reminds him of the ice and snow at the South Pole. Poor thing, maybe he's thirsty."

(1) Put a check (✓) next to all the adjectives in the passage that apply to the penguin:

(   ) ⓐ speechless   (   ) ⓑ thirsty   (   ) ⓒ stout

(   ) ⓓ pompous   (   ) ⓔ delighted   (   ) ⓕ dirty

(   ) ⓖ curious   (   ) ⓗ strange   (   ) ⓘ pleased

(2) Despite its size, what does the Penguin look like?

The penguin looks like a _____, with its _____

_____ in front and its _____ behind.

Can you imagine a penguin in your house?

Characters
Mr. Popper's Penguins 3

25

Date   /   /

Name

Level
★★★

Score

/100

1 Read the passage and then answer the questions using words from the passage.

10 points per question

Carefully Mr. Popper began to fill the bathtub with cold water. This was a little difficult because the inquisitive bird kept reaching over and trying to bite the faucets with its sharp red beak. Finally, however, he succeeded in getting the tub all filled. Since the penguin kept looking over, Mr. Popper picked it up and dropped it in. The penguin seemed not to mind.

"Anyway, you're not shy," said Mr. Popper. "I guess you've got sort of used to playing around with all those explorers at the Pole."

When he thought the penguin had had enough of a bath, he drew out the stopper. He was just wondering what to do next when Janie and Bill burst in from school.

"Papa," they shouted together at the bathroom door. "What is it?"

"It's a South Pole penguin sent to me by Admiral Drake."

"Look!" said Bill. "It's marching."

The delighted penguin was indeed marching. With little pleased nods of his handsome black head, he was parading up and down inside of the bathtub. Sometimes he seemed to be counting the steps it took — six steps for the length, two steps for the width, six steps for the length again, and two more for the width.

(1) How did the penguin like its bath?

The penguin seemed _____.

(2) Why did Mr. Popper think the penguin was not shy?

Mr. Popper thought the penguin was not shy because it had gotten used to

_____ with all those _____.

(3) How did the penguin march?

The penguin marched with little _____

_____.

(4) What was the penguin doing while he was marching?

The penguin seemed to be _____ to get

from one end of the bathtub to the other.

2 Read the passage. Then answer the questions below by circling the correct word.

10 points per question

"For such a big bird, he takes awfully small steps," said Bill.

"And look how his little black coat drags behind. It almost looks as if it were too big for him," said Janie.

But the penguin was tired of marching. This time, when it got to the end of the tub, it decided to jump up the slippery curve. Then it turned, and with outstretched flippers, tobogganed down on its white stomach. They could see that those flippers, which were black on the outside, like the sleeves of a tailcoat, were white underneath.

"*Gook! Gook!*" said the penguin, trying its new game again and again.

"What's his name, Papa?" asked Janie.

"*Gook! Gook!*" said the penguin, sliding once more on his glossy white stomach.

"It sounds something like 'Cook,'" said Mr. Popper. "Why that's it, of course. We'll call him Cook — Captain Cook."

(1) What color is the penguin's back? **Black** **White**

(2) What color are the outsides of the penguin's flippers? **Black** **White**

(3) What color is it underneath the penguin's flippers? **Black** **White**

(4) What color is the penguin's stomach? **Black** **White**

3 Read the passage. Then answer the question using words from the passage.

20 points

"Call who Captain Cook?" asked Mrs. Popper. …

"Why, the penguin," said Mr. Popper. "I was just saying," he went on, as Mrs. Popper sat down suddenly on the floor to recover from her surprise, "that we'd name him after Captain Cook. He was a famous English explorer who lived about the time of the American Revolution. He sailed all over where no one had ever been before. He didn't actually get to the South Pole, of course, but he made a lot of important scientific discoveries about the Antarctic regions. He was a brave man and a kind leader. So I think Captain Cook would be a very suitable name for our penguin here."

The main idea of this passage is that

_____ would be a very

_____ for the penguin.

Do you have a pet?
If so, what's your pet's name?

Characters
Mr. Popper's Penguins 4

26

Level
★★★

Date
/ /

Name

Score
/100

1 Read the passage and then answer the questions below.

10 points per question

> "*Gork!*" said Captain Cook, suddenly getting lively again. With a flap of his flippers he jumped from the tub to the washstand, and stood there for a minute surveying the floor. Then he jumped down, walked over to Mrs. Popper, and began to peck her ankle.
>
> "Stop him, Papa!" screamed Mrs. Popper, retreating into the hallway with Captain Cook after her, and Mr. Popper and the children following. In the living room she paused. So did Captain Cook, for he was delighted with the room.
>
> Now a penguin may look very strange in a living room, but a living room looks very strange to a penguin. Even Mrs. Popper had to smile as they watched Captain Cook, with the light of curiosity in his excited circular eyes, and his black tailcoat dragging pompously behind his little pinkish feet, strut from one upholstered chair to another, pecking at each to see what it was made of. Then he turned suddenly and marched out to the kitchen.
>
> "Maybe he's hungry," said Janie.
>
> Captain Cook immediately marched up to the refrigerator.

(1) What did Captain Cook do after he jumped down from the washstand?

Captain Cook _____, and began _____

_____.

(2) Why did Captain Cook pause in the living room?

Captain Cook paused in the living room because he was _____

_____.

(3) How did Captain Cook strut from one chair to the other?

Captain Cook strutted with the _____ in his excited circular

eyes and his _____ pompously _____

_____.

(4) What is the main idea of the paragraph in gray? Put a check (✓) next to the correct idea below.

( ) ⓐ The penguin was curious about the living room.

( ) ⓑ Mrs. Popper smiled.

( ) ⓒ The penguin strutted around.

"*Gork?*" he inquired, turning to slant his head wisely at Mrs. Popper, and look pleadingly with his right eye.

"He certainly is cute," she said. "I guess I'll have to forgive him for biting my ankle. He probably only did it out of curiosity. Anyway, he's a nice clean-looking bird."

"*Ork?*" repeated the penguin, nibbling at the metal handle of the refrigerator with his upstretched beak.

Mr. Popper opened the door for him, and Captain Cook stood very high and leaned his sleek black head back so he could see inside. Now that Mr. Popper's work was over for the winter, the icebox was not quite so full as usual, but the penguin did not know that.

"What do you suppose he likes to eat?" asked Mrs. Popper.

"Let's see," said Mr. Popper, as he removed all the food and set it on the kitchen table. "Now then Captain Cook, take a look."

The penguin jumped up onto a chair and from there onto the edge of the table, flapping his flippers again to recover his balance. Then he walked solemnly around the table, and between the dishes of food, inspecting everything with the greatest interest, though he touched nothing. Finally, he stood very still, very erect, raised his beak to point at the ceiling, and made a loud, almost purring sound. "*O-r-r-r-h, o-r-r-r-h,*" he trilled.

(1) How did the Popper family know that Captain Cook wanted to open the refrigerator?

They knew that Captain Cook wanted to open the refrigerator because he was

_____ at the _____ of the refrigerator with his

_____.

(2) Was Mrs. Popper still angry at the penguin for biting her ankle? Why or why not?

Mrs. Popper _____ angry at the penguin, because she thought he

probably only _____.

(3) Why was the icebox not as full as usual?

The icebox was not as full as usual because _____

_____.

(4) How did Captain Cook inspect the food?

Captain Cook walked _____

around the table, inspecting everything

with the _____,

but he _____ nothing.

If you want to know more about *Mr. Popper's Penguins,* read the rest of the book!

Reading Comprehension
Many Moons 1

Level
★★★

Date   /   /

Name

Score
/100

1 Read the passage from *Many Moons* by James Thurber. Then answer the questions below.

The Jester came bounding into the throne room in his motley* and his cap and bells, and sat at the foot of the throne.

"What can I do for you, your Majesty?" asked the Court Jester.

"Nobody can do anything for me," said the King mournfully. "The Princess Lenore wants the moon, and she cannot be well until she gets it, but nobody can get it for her. Every time I ask anybody for the moon, it gets larger and farther away. There is nothing you can do for me except play on your lute. Something sad."

"How big do they say the moon is," asked the Court Jester, "and how far away?"

"The Lord High Chamberlain says it is 35,000 miles away, and bigger than the Princess Lenore's room," said the King. "The Royal Wizard says it is 150,000 miles away and twice as big as the palace. The Royal Mathematician says it is 300,000 miles away and half the size of this kingdom."

*motley – a woolen coat of mixed colors

(1) Complete the statement using words from passage only.

10 points per question

① Who wanted the moon?

The _____ the moon.

② What did the King want the Jester to do?

The King wanted the Jester to _____ something _____ on his _____.

(2) Fill out the chart below with information from the passage.

10 points per question

Advisor	How Far Away They Believe the Moon Is	Size of Moon
The Lord High Chamberlain	①	Bigger than Lenore's room
②	150,000 miles	Twice as big as the palace
The Royal Mathematician	300,000 miles	③

2 Read the passage and answer the questions below using words from the passage.

10 points per question

> The Court Jester strummed on his lute for a little while. "They are all wise men," he said, "and so they must all be right. If they are all right, then the moon must be just as large and as far away as each person thinks it is. The thing to do is find out how big the Princess Lenore thinks it is, and how far away."
>
> "I never thought of that," said the King.
>
> "I will go and ask her, your Majesty," said the Court Jester. And he crept softly into the little girl's room.
>
> The Princess Lenore was awake, and she was glad to see the Court Jester, but her face was very pale and her voice was very weak.
>
> "Have you brought the moon to me?" she asked.
>
> "Not yet," said the Court Jester, "but I will get it for you right away. How big do you think it is?"
>
> "It is just a little smaller than my thumbnail," she said, "for when I hold my thumbnail up at the moon, it just covers it."
>
> "And how far away is it?" asked the Court Jester.
>
> "It is not as high as the big tree outside my window," said the Princess, "for sometimes it gets caught in the top branches."

(1) Which wise man did the Jester say was right?

The Jester said they are all wise men, _____.

(2) What did the Jester want to ask the Princess?

The Jester wanted to ask the Princess _____ she thought the moon was,

and _____.

(3) In what condition did the Jester find the Princess?

Princess Lenore was _____, but her face was _____ and her voice

was _____.

(4) How big did the Princess think the moon was?

The Princess thought the moon was _____ her

_____.

(5) Why did the Princess think this?

The Princess thought this because when she held

her _____,

it just covered it.

How big do *you* think the moon is?

Reading Comprehension
Many Moons 2

28

Level ★★★

Date / /

Name

Score /100

1 Read the passage. Then identify the statements below as **T** (true) or **F** (false) according to the passage.

10 points per question

"It will be very easy to get the moon for you," said the Court Jester. "I will climb the tree tonight and when it gets caught in the top branches and bring it to you."

Then he thought of something else. "What is the moon made of, Princess?" he asked.

"Oh," she said, "it's made of gold of course, silly."

The Court Jester left the Princess Lenore's room and went to see the Royal Goldsmith. He had the Royal Goldsmith make a tiny round golden moon just a little smaller than the thumbnail of the Princess Lenore. Then he had him string it on a golden chain so the Princess could wear it around her neck.

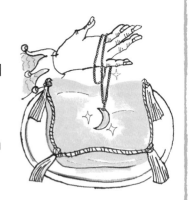

"What is this thing I have made?" asked the Royal Goldsmith when he had finished it.

"You have made the moon," said the Court Jester.

(1)   The Jester said it would be very easy to get the Moon for the Princess.   **T**   **F**

(2)   The Princess said the moon was made of gold.   **T**   **F**

(3)   The Jester climbed a tree to get the Moon for the Princess.   **T**   **F**

(4)   The Royal Goldsmith knew what he had made.   **T**   **F**

(5)   The Royal Goldsmith made a necklace for the Princess.   **T**   **F**

(6)   The Royal Goldsmith made a real moon for the Princess.   **T**   **F**

2 Read the passage. Then identify the statements below as **T** (true) or **F** (false) according to the passage.

5 points per question

"That is the moon."

"But the moon," said the Royal Goldsmith, "is 500,000 miles away and is made of bronze and is round like a marble."

"That's what you think," said the Court Jester as he went away with the moon.

The Court Jester took the moon to the Princess Lenore, and she was overjoyed. The next day she was well again and could get up and go out in the gardens to play.

(1) The Royal Goldsmith thought the moon was made of silver.   **T**   **F**

(2) The Court Jester thought the moon was made of bronze.   **T**   **F**

(3) The Court Jester's gift upset the Princess Lenore.   **T**   **F**

(4) The Princess Lenore was healthy again.   **T**   **F**

3 Read the passage and then answer the question below with words from the passage.

20 points

But the King's worries were not yet over. He knew that the moon would shine in the sky again that night, and he did not want the Princess Lenore to see it. If she did, she would know that the moon she wore on a chain around her neck was not the real moon.

The main idea of this passage is that the King's _____
_____.

This king worries a lot!

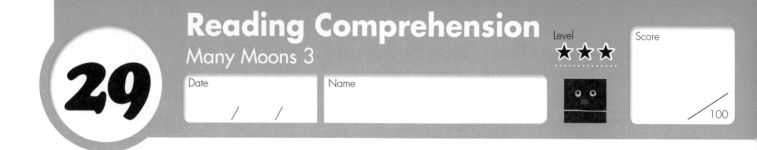

Reading Comprehension
Many Moons 3

29

Level ★★★

Date   /   /

Name

Score
/100

1 Read the passage. Then answer the questions below.

So the King sent for the Lord High Chamberlain and said, "We must keep the Princess Lenore from seeing the moon when it shines in the sky tonight. Think of something."

The Lord High Chamberlain tapped his forehead with his fingers thoughtfully and said, "I know just the thing. We can make some dark glasses for the Princess Lenore. We can make them so dark that she will not be able to see anything at all through them. Then she will not be able to see the moon when it shines in the sky."

This made the King very angry, and he shook his head from side to side. "If she wore dark glasses, she would bump into things," he said, "and then she would be ill again."

(1) Identify the statements below as **T** (true) or **F** (false) according to the passage.

10 points per question

① The Lord High Chamberlain had dark glasses.   **T**   **F**

② The Lord High Chamberlain had a good solution to the problem.   **T**   **F**

(2) Answer the questions below using information from the passage.

10 points per question

① What did the King want the Lord High Chamberlain to help him do?

The King wanted the Lord High Chamberlain to help him keep _____

_____ when it shined _____ that night.

② What did the King think would be the effect of giving the Princess Lenore dark glasses?

The King thought that if the Princess Lenore wore dark glasses, _____

_____ and be _____.

2 Read the passage and then answer the questions below using words from the passage.

15 points per question

So he sent the Lord High Chamberlain away and called the Royal Wizard.

"We must hide the moon," said the King, "so that the Princess Lenore will not see it when it shines in the sky tonight. How are we going to do that?"

The Royal Wizard stood on his hands, and then he stood on his head, and then he stood on his feet again.

"I know what we can do," he said. "We can stretch some black velvet curtains on poles. The curtains will cover all the palace gardens like a circus tent, and then Princess Lenore will not be able to see through them, so she will not see the moon in the sky."

The King was so angry at this that he waved his arms around. "Black velvet curtains would keep out the air," he said. "The Princess Lenore would not be able to breathe, and she would be ill again."

(1) What happened after the King asked the Royal Wizard for advice?

The Royal Wizard _____, and then _____

_____, and then _____.

(2) What is the paragraph in gray mostly about?

The Royal Wizard said that they could _____

_____ so that the Princess Lenore could not _____

_____ and _____ in the sky.

(3) How did the King react to the Royal Wizard's idea?

The King was _____.

(4) What would be the effect of putting black velvet curtains around the palace?

If the Wizard put up black velvet curtains around the palace, the Princess

Lenore _____

_____.

This is another bad solution!

Reading Comprehension
Many Moons 4

30

Level ★★★

Date / /

Name

Score

/ 100

1 Read the passage and then answer the questions below.

20 points per question

> So he sent the Royal Wizard away and summoned the Royal Mathematician. ...
>
> The Royal Mathematician walked around in a circle, and then he walked around in a square, and then he stood still. "I have it!" he said.
>
> "We can set off fireworks in the gardens every night. We will make a lot of silver fountains and golden cascades, and when they go off, they will fill the sky with so many sparks that it will be as light as day and the Princess Lenore will not be able to see the moon."
>
> The King flew into such a rage that he began jumping up and down. "Fireworks would keep the Princess Lenore awake," he said. "She would not get any sleep at all and she would be ill again." So the King sent the Royal Mathematician away.
>
> When he looked up again, it was dark outside and he saw the bright rim of the moon just peeping over the horizon. He jumped up in great fright and rang for the Court Jester. The Court Jester came bounding into the room and sat down at the foot of the throne.

(1) What did the Royal Mathematician do when the King summoned him?

The Royal Mathematician _____

_____.

(2) Put a check (✓) next to all of the phrases that apply to the King.

( ) ⓐ came bounding into the room

( ) ⓑ flew into a rage

( ) ⓒ stood still

( ) ⓓ jumped up in great fright

(3) What caused the King to jump up in a great fright?

The King saw _____

_____.

2 Read the passage and then answer the questions below.

"What can I do for you, your Majesty?" he asked.

"Nobody can do anything for me," said the King mournfully. "The moon is coming up again. It will shine into the Princess Lenore's bedroom, and she will know it is still in the sky and that she does not wear it on a golden chain around her neck. Play me something on your lute, something very sad, for when the Princess sees the moon, she will be ill again."

The Court Jester strummed on his lute. "What do your wise men say?" he asked.

"They can think of no way to hide the moon that will not make the Princess Lenore ill," said the King.

The Court Jester played another song, very softly. "Your wise men know everything," he said, "and if they cannot hide the moon, then it cannot be hidden."

The King put his head in his hands again and sighed.

(1) Why was the King sad?

The King was sad because the moon was _____, and

the Princess Lenore would know that the moon was _____ and

that she did not _____ around her neck.

(2) How could the Jester help the King feel better?

The Jester could help the King by playing _____ on his

_____.

(3) What have the wise men said to the King?

The wise men could think of _____

_____.

(4) What did the Jester say about the King's wise men?

The Jester said that the King's _____.

Will the King find a good solution?
Try reading the rest of *Many Moons* to find out!

Reading Comprehension
The Wizard of Oz 1

31

Level ★★★

Date   /   /

Name

Score   /100

1 Read the passage from *The Wizard of Oz* by L. Frank Baum. Then identify the statements below as **T** (true) or **F** (false) according to the passage.

10 points per question

Uncle Henry never laughed. He worked hard from morning till night and did not know what joy was. He was gray also, from his long beard to his rough boots, and he looked stern and solemn, and rarely spoke.

It was Toto that made Dorothy laugh, and saved her from growing as gray as her other surroundings. Toto was not gray; he was a little black dog, with long silky hair and small black eyes that twinkled merrily on either side of his funny, wee nose. Toto played all day long, and Dorothy played with him, and loved him dearly.

Today, however, they were not playing. Uncle Henry sat upon the doorstep and looked anxiously at the sky, which was even grayer than usual. Dorothy stood in the door with Toto in her arms, and looked at the sky too. Aunt Em was washing the dishes.

(1) Uncle Henry's eyes twinkled when he laughed.   **T**   **F**

(2) Uncle Henry was solemn and gray.   **T**   **F**

(3) Toto made Dorothy laugh.   **T**   **F**

(4) Toto had smooth hair and a small nose.   **T**   **F**

(5) Toto was as gray as the surroundings.   **T**   **F**

(6) The sky was gray.   **T**   **F**

2 Read the passage below. Then pick the phrase that best expresses the main idea.

10 points

From the far north they heard a low wail of the wind, and Uncle Henry and Dorothy could see where the long grass bowed in waves before the coming storm. There now came a sharp whistling in the air from the south, and as they turned their eyes that way they saw ripples in the grass coming from that direction also.

ⓐ Uncle Henry and Dorothy   ⓑ The Coming Storm

ⓒ The Rippling Grass   ⓓ The Bowing Grass   (   )

3 Read the passage. Then answer the questions below using words from the passage.

10 points per question

Suddenly Uncle Henry stood up.

"There's a cyclone coming, Em," he called to his wife. "I'll go look after the stock." Then he ran toward the sheds where the cows and horses were kept.

Aunt Em dropped her work and came to the door. One glance told her of the danger close at hand.

"Quick, Dorothy!" she screamed. "Run for the cellar!"

Toto jumped out of Dorothy's arms and hid under the bed, and the girl started to get him. Aunt Em, badly frightened, threw open the trap door in the floor and climbed down the ladder into the small, dark hole. Dorothy caught Toto at last and started to follow her aunt.

(1) What did Uncle Henry call to Aunt Em?

Uncle Henry called out, "_____."

(2) Where did Uncle Henry keep his stock?

Uncle Henry kept his stock in _____.

(3) How did Aunt Em react to Uncle Henry's news?

Upon hearing the news, Aunt Em screamed to _____,

threw open _____, and

climbed _____ into the cellar.

Something exciting is in the air!

Reading Comprehension
The Wizard of Oz 2

32

Level ★★★

Date   /   /

Name

Score

/100

1 Read the passage. Then answer the questions below.

When she was halfway across the room there came a great shriek from the wind, and the house shook so hard that she lost her footing and sat down suddenly upon the floor.

Then a strange thing happened.

The house whirled around two or three times and rose slowly through the air. Dorothy felt as if she were going up in a balloon.

The north and south winds met where the house stood, and made it the exact center of the cyclone. In the middle of a cyclone the air is generally still, but the great pressure of the wind on every side of the house raised it up higher and higher, until it was at the very top of the cyclone; and there it remained and was carried miles and miles away as easily as you could carry a feather.

It was very dark, and the wind howled horribly around her, but Dorothy found she was riding quite easily. After the first few whirls around, and one other time when the house tipped badly, she felt as if she were being rocked gently, like a baby in a cradle.

(1) Fill in the chart below with information from the passage.

4 points per question

The Power of the Wind
gave a great ① _____
② _____ the house hard
③ _____ the house around ④ _____ times
⑤ _____ the house up ⑥ _____
⑦ _____ horribly

(2) Answer the questions below using words from the passage.

11 points per question

① Where did the north and south winds meet?

The north and south winds met _____.

② After the house tipped badly, how did Dorothy find the ride inside the house?

Dorothy felt as if she were _____, like _____

_____.

2 Read the passage. Then fill in the chart using words from the passage to contrast the characters' reactions to the wind.

4 points per question

Toto did not like it. He ran about the room, now here, now there, barking loudly; but Dorothy sat quite still on the floor and waited to see what would happen.

Once Toto got too near the open trap door, and fell in; and at first the little girl thought she had lost him. But soon she saw one of his ears sticking up through the hole, for the strong pressure of the air was keeping him up so that he could not fall. She crept to the hole, caught Toto by the ear, and dragged him into the room again, afterward closing the trap door so that no more accidents could happen.

The Power of the Wind		
Toto	ran ① _____, barking ② _____	fell in ③ _____
Dorothy	④ _____ on the floor	caught ⑤ _____ and closed the trap door

3 Read the passage. Then answer the questions below using words from the passage.

10 points per question

Hour after hour passed away, and slowly Dorothy got over her fright; but she felt quite lonely, and the wind shrieked so loudly all about her that she nearly became deaf. At first she had wondered if she would be dashed to pieces when the house fell again; but as the hours passed and nothing terrible happened, she stopped worrying and resolved to wait calmly and see what the future would bring.

(1) How did Dorothy feel after she got over her fright?

After she got over her fright, she felt _____.

(2) What caused Dorothy to nearly become deaf?

She nearly became deaf because _____

_____.

(3) What was the effect of hours passing and nothing terrible happening?

As the hours passed, Dorothy stopped

_____

_____

_____.

What scary thing have you found out wasn't so scary after all?

© Kumon Publishing Co., Ltd.   65

Reading Comprehension
The Wizard of Oz 3

33

Level
★★★

Date
/   /

Name

Score
/100

1 Read the passage. Then identify the statements below as **T** (true) or **F** (false) according to the passage.

10 points per question

At last she crawled over the swaying floor to her bed, and lay down upon it; and Toto followed and lay down beside her.

In spite of the swaying of the house and the wailing of the wind, Dorothy soon closed her eyes and fell fast asleep.

2. THE COUNCIL WITH THE MUNCHKINS

She was awakened by a shock, so sudden and severe that if Dorothy had not been lying on the soft bed she might have been hurt. As it was, the jar made her catch her breath and wonder what had happened; and Toto put his cold little nose into her face and whined dismally. Dorothy sat up and noticed that the house was not moving; nor was it dark, for the bright sunshine came in at the window, flooding the little room. She sprang from her bed and with Toto at her heels ran and opened the door.

The little girl gave a cry of amazement and looked about her, her eyes growing bigger and bigger at the wonderful sights she saw.

(1) The wind screamed and the house rocked.   T   F

(2) Dorothy woke up gradually and gently.   T   F

(3) The landing of the house was jarring and shocking.   T   F

(4) Toto was happy to have landed.   T   F

(5) Dorothy did not pay attention to her new surroundings.   T   F

2 Read the passage and then answer the questions below.

10 points per question

> The cyclone had set the house down very gently — for a cyclone — in the midst of a country of marvelous beauty. There were lovely patches of greensward* all about, with stately trees bearing rich and luscious fruits. Banks of gorgeous flowers were on every hand, and birds with rare and brilliant plumage sang and fluttered in the trees and bushes. A little way off was a small brook, rushing and sparkling along between green banks, and murmuring in a voice very grateful to a little girl who had lived so long on the dry, gray prairies.
>
> While she stood looking eagerly at the strange and beautiful sights, she noticed coming toward her a group of the queerest people she had ever seen. They were not as big as the grown folk she had always been used to; but neither were they very small. In fact, they seemed about as tall as Dorothy, who was a well-grown child for her age, although they were, so far as looks go, many years older.

greensward – turf that is green with growing grass

(1) What is the main idea of the paragraph in gray? Put a check (✓) next to the correct idea below.

( ) ⓐ Dorothy was in a cyclone.

( ) ⓑ The prairies Dorothy left behind were dry and gray.

( ) ⓒ Dorothy had arrived in a beautiful new land.

(2) Describe the appearance of the group of people that approached Dorothy using words from the passage.

The people were not _____ that Dorothy was used

to, but they looked _____ than Dorothy or other children.

3 Identify the statements as **T** (true) or **F** (false) according to the passage.

10 points per question

(1) The whirlwind lowered the house more peacefully than expected.   **T**   **F**

(2) There were majestic trees filled with delicious fruits.   **T**   **F**

(3) The birds had dull, gray feathers and sat quietly on the prairie.   **T**   **F**

> You can see strange and beautiful sights every time you pick up a book.

Reading Comprehension
The Wizard of Oz 4

34

Level ★★★

Date / /

Name

Score

/100

1 Read the passage and then answer the questions below.

Three were men and one a woman, and all were oddly dressed. …

When these people drew near the house where Dorothy was standing in the doorway, they paused and whispered among themselves, as if afraid to come farther. But the little old woman walked up to Dorothy, made a low bow and said, in a sweet voice:

"You are welcome, most noble Sorceress, to the land of the Munchkins. We are so grateful to you for having killed the Wicked Witch of the East, and for setting our people free from bondage."

Dorothy listened to this speech with wonder. What could the little woman possibly mean by calling her a sorceress, and saying she had killed the Wicked Witch of the East? Dorothy was an innocent, harmless little girl, who had been carried by a cyclone many miles from home; and she had never killed anything in all her life.

But the little woman evidently expected her to answer; so Dorothy said, with hesitation, "You are very kind, but there must be some mistake. I have not killed anything."

(1) Identify the statements below as **T** (true) or **F** (false) according to the passage.   10 points per question

① The unusually dressed people muttered nervously.   **T**   **F**

② The little old woman made Dorothy feel unwelcome.   **T**   **F**

③ Dorothy answered the little woman immediately.   **T**   **F**

(2) Answer the questions below using words from the passage.   10 points per question

① What was one effect of the Wicked Witch of the East being killed?

When the Wicked Witch of the East was killed, the Munchkins were set free

_____.

② What is the main idea of the paragraph in gray? Put a check (✓) next to the correct idea.

( ) ⓐ Dorothy is the Wicked Witch of the East.

( ) ⓑ Dorothy is confused by what the Munchkin woman said to her.

( ) ⓒ Dorothy was far from home.

2 Read the passage and then answer the questions below.

"Your house did, anyway," replied the little old woman, with a laugh, "and that is the same thing. See!" she continued, pointing to the corner of the house. "There are her two feet, still sticking out from under a block of wood."

Dorothy looked, and gave a little cry of fright. There, indeed, just under the corner of the great beam the house rested on, two feet were sticking out, shod in silver shoes with pointed toes.

"Oh, dear! Oh, dear!" cried Dorothy, clasping her hands together in dismay. "The house must have fallen on her. Whatever shall we do?"

"There is nothing to be done," said the little woman calmly.

"But who was she?" asked Dorothy.

"She was the Wicked Witch of the East, as I said," answered the little woman. "She has held all the Munchkins in bondage for many years, making them slave for her night and day. Now they are all set free, and are grateful to you for the favor."

"Who are the Munchkins?" inquired Dorothy.

"They are the people who live in the land of the East where the Wicked Witch ruled."

(1) What stuck out from under the beam of Dorothy's house?

Two feet, shod _____, stuck

out from under the block of wood.

(2) What did Dorothy realize must have happened to the Wicked Witch?

Dororthy realized that her house _____.

(3) What did the Wicked Witch of the East do to the Munchkins?

The Wicked Witch of the East held them in _____ and made them

_____.

(4) Who are the Munchkins?

The Munchkins are _____

_____.

(5) Put a check (✓) next to all of the phrases that apply to the little old woman.

( ) ⓐ replied with a laugh   ( ) ⓑ spoke calmly

( ) ⓒ gave a little cry of fright   ( ) ⓓ set the Munchkins free

( ) ⓔ wore silver shoes with pointed toes

Try reading the entire book, *The Wizard of Oz* by L. Frank Baum.
If you like it, there are many other books in the series!

35
Review

Level ★★

Score
/100

Date / /

Name

1 Pick the correct word from the box to complete each sentence below.

8 points per question

| foundation | whirled | symbols | discoveries | curious |

(1) Our dog was _____ about the contents or our shopping bag.

(2) Jin's balloon was _____ away by the wind.

(3) Concrete makes a better _____ than wood because it lasts longer.

(4) The 50 stars on the American flag are _____ of the 50 states.

(5) Captain Cook made many important _____ on his travels.

2 Read the passage. Then identify the statements below as **T** (true) or **F** (false) according to the passage.

5 points per question

There are both human-made and natural materials that can be recycled. The human-made materials include paper, plastic, glass, and metal, which must be delivered to special factories for recycling. The natural materials include kitchen and garden wastes, such as vegetable parings and lawn clippings. These can be recycled in your backyard. Natural materials will break down and return to the soil. Human-made materials almost never break down on their own.

(1) Plastic must be taken to a factory for recycling. **T** **F**

(2) Kitchen waste can be recycled in the backyard. **T** **F**

(3) Vegetable pairings will not break down on their own. **T** **F**

(4) Paper is considered a natural material. **T** **F**

3 Complete the crossword puzzle using the sentences below as clues.
Use capital letters.

5 points per question

```
(5)
 C                              (7)
                                 D
(1) U            R    B
                                      (8)
                                       M
(2)  R      P              G
          (6)
     (3)  C        P              T

                    (4)  S         U

          Y
```

ACROSS

(1) The noise was so loud it was almost ___?___.

(2) Our dogs ___?___ all of our roses in the garden yesterday.

(3) I got first place and beat out all of my ___?___ at the track meet!

(4) The ___?___ to the problem was easy once he thought about it.

DOWN

(5) ___?___ on the new school began today.

(6) The only ___?___ used in the United States today is the dollar.

(7) My sister was ___?___ by all the presents she got for her birthday.

(8) The magician was very ___?___. He disappeared from the stage!

Almost done!

36 Review

Level ★★

Score

/100

Date / /

Name

1 Read the passage, from *Mr. Popper's Penguins* by Florence Atwater, and then answer the questions below.

20 points per question

> Mrs. Popper had gone marketing for canned shrimps for the penguin, so that Mr. Popper was alone in the kitchen to explain to the service man what he wanted done to the refrigerator.
>
> The service man put his tool bag down on the floor, looked at the refrigerator, and then at Mr. Popper, who, to tell the truth, had not shaved yet and was not very tidy.
>
> "Mister," he said, "you don't need no ventilating holes in that there door."
>
> "It's my icebox, and I want some holes bored in the door," said Mr. Popper.
>
> They argued about it for quite a while. Mr. Popper knew that to get the service man to do what he wanted, all he had to do was explain that he was going to keep a live penguin in the icebox, and that he wanted his pet to have plenty of fresh air, even though the door was closed all night. He felt a little stubborn about explaining, however. He didn't want to discuss Captain Cook with this unsymphathetic service man, who was already staring at Mr. Popper as if he thought Mr. Popper was not quite right in his head.

(1) Why was Mr. Popper alone in the kitchen with the service man?

Mr. Popper was alone in the kitchen because Mrs. Popper had _____

_____.

(2) What caused Mr. Popper to look untidy?

Mr. Popper looked untidy because he _____.

(3) What is the main idea of the passage in gray? Put a check (✓) next to the correct idea below.

(　)　ⓐ Mr. Popper was not quite right in the head.

(　)　ⓑ Mr. Popper argued about wanting to bore holes in the door.

(　)　ⓒ Mr. Popper felt stubborn.

(　)　ⓓ Mr. Popper liked the service man.

2 Read the passage and then answer the questions below.

> "Come on, do what I said," said Mr. Popper. "I'm paying you for it."
>
> "With what?" asked the service man.
>
> Mr. Popper gave him a five-dollar bill. It made him a little sad to think how many beans it would have bought for Mrs. Popper and the children.
>
> The service man examined the bill carefully as if he didn't trust Mr. Popper too much. But at last he put it in his pocket, took a drill from his tool bag, and made five small holes in a neat pattern on the refrigerator door.
>
> "Now," said Mr. Popper, "don't get up. Wait a minute. There is one more thing."
>
> "Now what?" said the service man. "I suppose now you want me to take the door off its hinges to let in a little more air. Or do you want me to make a radio set out of your icebox?"
>
> "Don't get funny," said Mr. Popper indignantly. "That is no way to talk. Believe it or not, I know what I'm doing. I mean, having you do. I want you to fix an extra handle inside of that box so it can be opened from the inside of the box."

(1) Why was Mr. Popper a little sad to give the service man the five dollars?

Mr. Popper was a little sad because he was thinking about _____

_____ the five dollars would have _____

_____.

(2) How could Mr. Popper tell that the service man did not trust him too much?

Mr. Popper could tell that the service man did not trust him too much because the

service man _____.

(3) What made Mr. Popper tell the service man not to be funny?

Mr. Popper told the service man not to be funny after he asked Mr. Popper if he

wanted to make a _____ out of the _____.

(4) What was the extra thing that Mr. Popper wanted?

Mr. Popper wanted the service man to _____

of the icebox.

Wow! Congratulations!!!

1 Vocabulary
pp 2,3

1 (1) very badly / weeks before tryouts began
  (2) restless
  (3) fastest
  (4) bigger and stronger
  (5) swiftly

2 (1) big / biggest
  (2) useful / useless
  (3) swift / swiftly
  (4) heavy / heavier
  (5) cheerful / cheerfully
  (6) careless / careful

3 (1) ⓒ   (2) ⓖ
  (3) ⓔ   (4) ⓕ
  (5) ⓓ   (6) ⓐ
  (7) ⓑ

2 Vocabulary
pp 4,5

1 (1) ① overcrowding
    ② recycle
    ③ reusable
  (2) ① up to four-and-a-half pounds of trash per day
    ② overcrowding in our landfills

2 (1) reuse
  (2) usable
  (3) overcrowded
  (4) recycle
  (5) unbelievable
  (6) unfolded

3

3 Defining Words by Context
pp 6,7

1 (1) ① competition
    ② recreation
    ③ invention
    ④ inscription
  (2) big medal / free trip to space camp

2 (1) all vacation long
  (2) begging for her attention
  (3) start building her project
  (4) construction / due early in the school year

3 (1) attention
  (2) competition
  (3) invention
  (4) construction
  (5) recreation

4 Defining Words by Context
pp 8,9

1 (1) ① enormous
    ② suspicious
    ③ dangerous
    ④ anxious
  (2) funny / serious matter

2 (1) nervous
  (2) run / tripped and fell over his big shoes
  (3) curious / missing elephant

3 (1) nervous
  (2) dangerous
  (3) famous
  (4) enormous
  (5) curious

5 Vocabulary Review pp 10, 11

1 (1) swiftly
(2) recycle
(3) famous
(4) dangerous
(5) invention
(6) construction

2 (1) recreation
(2) cheerfully
(3) reusable
(4) science
(5) anxious

3 (1) NERVOUSLY
(2) ASTRONAUT
(3) VACATION
(4) FAMOUS
(5) UNBELIEVABLE
(6) SUSPICIOUS
(7) ATTENTION
(8) CURIOUS

6 Who/What/When/Where/Why/How pp 12, 13

1 (1) Mint
(2) coins
(3) need its own coins
(4) 1792

2 (1) trouble / coins for the country
(2) coin currency
(3) mixtures of metals
(4) picture / model
(5) famous historical person

7 Who/What/When/Where/Why/How pp 14, 15

1 (1) everyone should participate
(2) every Wednesday
(3) to take out the garbage
(4) Patty / shovel the driveway

2 (1) checked in the pantry
(2) her recipe needed two cans
(3) make less pasta / less sauce
(4) use the stove with her help
(5) to the curb to be recycled

8 Who/What/When/Where/Why/How pp 16, 17

1 (1) make very low notes
(2) even lower sound
(3) sister Lisa
(4) blows air into
(5) in the spring

2 (1) dancing to the melodies / tapping their feet
(2) brass instruments / piano
(3) loves entertaining
(4) compete / other trombone players
(5) every Tuesday afternoon

9 Who/What/When/Where/Why/How pp 18, 19

1 (1) hamburger or chicken
(2) trapping bugs
(3) in North Carolina and South Carolina
(4) less bog land now

2 (1) white flowers bloom
(2) to drink juice from them
(3) while drinking / to close over the bug
(4) After the bug is caught
(5) nutrients
(6) taken Venus flytraps from their native bogs

10 Vocabulary Review
pp 20,21

1 (1) nervous
(2) instrument
(3) locations
(4) native
(5) currency

2 (1) mixture
(2) saxophone
(3) bog
(4) historical
(5) designers

3 (1) ENTERTAIN
(2) PARTICIPATE
(3) ENGRAVED
(4) SOLUTION
(5) NUTRIENTS
(6) SCIENTISTS
(7) ENDANGERED
(8) MELODY

11 True or False
pp 22,23

1 (1) materials
(2) concrete
(3) foundation
(4) construct

2 (1) T　(2) F　(3) T　(4) T　(5) F

3 (1) F　(2) T　(3) F　(4) T

4 (1) shortened to 5,200 miles
(2) pay a heavy toll

12 True or False
pp 24,25

1 (1) spectators
(2) opponent(s)
(3) dribble
(4) teammate

2 (1) F　(2) T　(3) F　(4) T

3 (1) T　(2) T　(3) F　(4) T　(5) F　(6) F

4 (1) T　(2) F

13 True or False
pp 26,27

1 (1) peaceful
(2) survive
(3) intruder
(4) defend

2 (1) F　(2) F　(3) T　(4) F　(5) F　(6) T

3 (1) T　(2) T　(3) F　(4) T　(5) F　(6) T

4 (1) in zoos
(2) only real enemy

14 Cause & Effect
pp 28,29

1 (1) drought / did not rain
(2) would die
(3) spread out / look for water
(4) scared many rabbits / destroyed many houses

2 (a) 6, (b) 1, (c) 5, (d) 7, (e) 3, (f) 4, (g) 2

15 Cause & Effect
pp 30,31

1 (1) under the Moon's protection
(2) terrible things / happen to
(3) was speechless / thought / spoke
(4) make sure / suffer anymore / apologize

2 (1) (b)
(2) (c)
(3) (a)

16 Cause & Effect
pp 32,33

1 (1) ⓐ, ⓒ, ⓓ
  (2) ⓐ, ⓒ

2 (1) ⓐ 1 ⓑ 4 ⓒ 2 ⓓ 3
  (2) plan / project a little earlier

17 Vocabulary Review
pp 34,35

1 (1) intruder
  (2) dribble
  (3) concrete
  (4) protection
  (5) apologized

2 (1) majestic
  (2) fierce
  (3) survive
  (4) urgent
  (5) terrible

3 (1) INSPECT
  (2) SPECTATORS
  (3) PEACEFUL
  (4) SIMPLE
  (5) OPPONENT
  (6) TEAMMATE
  (7) DISTURBED
  (8) MATERIAL

18 Main Idea
pp 36,37

1 (1) ① school bus
       ② walking
       ③ bus and train
       ④ car
  (2) ⓑ

2 (1) ⓐ
  (2) ⓒ

19 Main Idea
pp 38,39

1 (1) ① Italy
       ② Canada
       ③ Chad
       ④ (United States of) America
       ⑤ Mexico
  (2) ⓐ

2 (1) ① Olympics
       ② trouble
       ③ children's happiness
  (2) ⓒ

20 Main Idea
pp 40,41

1 (1) ⓐ
  (2) ⓐ
  (3) all lions are yellow

2 (1) ⓐ
  (2) ⓑ
  (3) ① Captain Max
       ② Dr. Bell
       ③ The Fastball Book

21 Main Idea
pp 42,43

1 (1) ⓒ
  (2) Can span a long distance
      Have two towers
      Make travel faster

2 (1) ⓑ
  (2) ⓐ
  (3) ① heavy
       ② earthquakes
       ③ sway
       ④ orange
       ⑤ easy

22 Vocabulary Review   pp 44,45

1 (1) span
(2) fuel
(3) pattern
(4) cultures
(5) ripples

2 (1) custom
(2) suspension
(3) mural
(4) architect
(5) poison

3 (1) TRANSPORTATION
(2) LABOR
(3) ARTICLE
(4) SYMBOL
(5) EARTHQUAKES
(6) CONSTRUCTION
(7) CARPOOL
(8) COMMUNITY

23 Characters   pp 46,47

1 (1) late September / little city of Stillwater
(2) painted over in the spring
(3) one day be the most famous person in Stillwater
(4) an untidy man

2 (1) T   (2) F   (3) F   (4) F   (5) T   (6) T

24 Characters   pp 48,49

1 (1) ⓐ, ⓑ, ⓒ
(2) ⓐ, ⓑ

2 (1) ⓑ, ⓒ, ⓓ, ⓖ, ⓗ, ⓘ
(2) little gentleman / smooth white waistcoat / long black tailcoat

25 Characters   pp 50,51

1 (1) not to mind
(2) playing around / explorers at the Pole
(3) pleased nods of his handsome black head
(4) counting the steps it took

2 (1) Black
(2) Black
(3) White
(4) White

3 Captain Cook / suitable name

26 Characters   pp 52,53

1 (1) walked over to Mrs. Popper / to peck her ankle
(2) delighted with the room
(3) light of curiosity / black tailcoat dragging / behind his little pinkish feet
(4) ⓐ

2 (1) nibbling / metal handle / upstretched beak
(2) was not / did it out of curiosity
(3) Mr. Popper's work was over for the winter
(4) solemnly / greatest interest / touched

27 Reading Comprehension   pp 54,55

1 (1) ① Princess Lenore wanted
② play / sad / lute
(2) ① 35,000 miles
② The Royal Wizard
③ Half the size of this kingdom

2 (1) and so they must all be right
(2) how big / how far away
(3) awake / very pale / very weak
(4) just a little smaller than / thumbnail
(5) thumbnail up at the moon

28 Reading Comprehension
pp 56,57

1 (1) T (2) T (3) F (4) F (5) T (6) F

2 (1) F (2) F (3) F (4) T

3 worries were not yet over

29 Reading Comprehension
pp 58,59

1 (1) ① F ② F
   (2) ① the Princess Lenore from seeing the moon /
      in the sky
   ② she would bump into things / ill again

2 (1) stood on his hands / he stood on his head /
      he stood on his feet again
   (2) stretch some black velvet curtains on poles /
      see through them / see the moon
   (3) so angry at this that he waved his arms
      around
   (4) would not be able to breathe, and she would
      be ill again

30 Reading Comprehension
pp 60,61

1 (1) walked around in a circle, and then he
      walked around in a square, and then he
      stood still
   (2) ⓑ, ⓓ
   (3) the bright rim of the moon just peeping over
      the horizon

2 (1) coming up again / still in the sky / wear it on a
      golden chain
   (2) something very sad / lute
   (3) no way to hide the moon that will not make
      the Princess Lenore ill
   (4) wise men know everything

31 Reading Comprehension
pp 62,63

1 (1) F (2) T (3) T (4) T (5) F (6) T

2 ⓑ

3 (1) There's a cyclone coming, Em
   (2) the sheds
   (3) Dorothy / the trap door in the floor / down the
      ladder

32 Reading Comprehension
pp 64,65

1 (1) ① shriek
      ② shook
      ③ whirled
      ④ two or three
      ⑤ raised
      ⑥ higher and higher
      ⑦ howled
   (2) ① where the house stood
      ② being rocked gently / a baby in a cradle

2 ① about the room
   ② loudly
   ③ the open trap door
   ④ sat quite still
   ⑤ Toto

3 (1) quite lonely
   (2) the wind shrieked so loudly all about her
   (3) worrying and resolved to wait calmly and see
      what the future would bring

33 Reading Comprehension
pp 66,67

1 (1) T (2) F (3) T (4) F (5) F

2 (1) ⓒ
   (2) as big as the grown folk / many years older

3 (1) T (2) T (3) F

(34) Reading Comprehension pp 68,69

1 (1) ① T   ② F   ③ F
   (2) ① from bondage
      ② ⓑ

2 (1) in silver shoes with pointed toes
   (2) must have fallen on her
   (3) bondage / slave for her night and day
   (4) the people who live in the land of the East
      where the Wicked Witch ruled

3 ⓐ, ⓑ

(35) Review pp 70,71

1 (1) curious
   (2) whirled
   (3) foundation
   (4) symbols
   (5) discoveries

2 (1) T   (2) T   (3) F   (4) F

3 (1) UNBEARABLE
   (2) TRAMPLED
   (3) COMPETITION
   (4) SOLUTION
   (5) CONSTRUCTION
   (6) CURRENCY
   (7) DELIGHTED
   (8) MYSTERIOUS

(36) Review pp 72,73

1 (1) gone marketing for canned shrimps for the
      penguin
   (2) had not shaved yet
   (3) ⓑ

2 (1) how many beans / bought for Mrs. Popper
      and the children
   (2) examined the bill carefully
   (3) radio set / icebox
   (4) fix an extra handle inside